YESTERYEAR IN ANNAPOLIS

The Statehouse, Annapolis, Maryland

Yesteryear in Annapolis

By *Harold N. Burdett*

Illustrated by *Eric Smith*

Tidewater Publishers

Cambridge   1974   *Maryland*

Copyright © 1974 by Tidewater Publishers

All Rights Reserved

No part of this book may be used or reproduced in any manner whatsoever without written permission except in the case of brief quotations embodied in critical articles and reviews. For information, address Tidewater Publishers, Cambridge, Maryland 21613

Library of Congress Cataloging in Publication Data

Burdett, Harold N   1933-
   Yesteryear in Annapolis.

   1. Annapolis--History.   I. Title.
F189.A6B87   975.2'56   74-26773
ISBN 0-87033-197-3

Printed and Bound in the United States of America

CONTENTS

Chapter		Page
	Frontispiece	ii
	Dedication	vii
	Biographical Data	ix
	Foreword	xi
I	The Man Who Put Annapolis on the Map	1
II	The Would-Be Buccaneer	3
III	The Tuesday Club	7
IV	The Unprincipled Parson	15
V	The Critical Clergyman	21
VI	Son of Discord	23
VII	The Versatile Gossip Diarist	27
VIII	Barnum's Big Lesson	33
IX	Old Joe Morgue	37
X	Bad Day at Crabtown	39
XI	The Governor's Lady	43
XII	The General Who Seized Annapolis	47
XIII	C'est la Guerre, You Rebs!	53
XIV	Days of Desperation	57
XV	The Russian Sailor Incident	63
XVI	Red Carpet Prisoners	67
XVII	The Last Captive	71
XVIII	Nightingale in a Hencoop	73
XIX	The Ghosts of Brice House	75
XX	The Unflappable Colonel of Maryland Avenue	79
XXI	The Spinsters' Pride	81

| XXII | Mark Twain's Visit to Annapolis | . . . . 85 |
| XXIII | The Plot to Steal the Naval Academy | . . . . . . 89 |

To the Memory

of

Nachman Burdett (1892-1956)

and

Lena Kobre Burdett (1896-1967)

BIOGRAPHICAL DATA

Harold N. Burdett was born in Washington, D.C., in 1933, and he has lived in Annapolis since 1966. He is the editor of *Maryland Free Lance,* a statewide political journal, and a contributing editor to *Emergency* and *Annapolitan* Magazines as well as a frequent contributor to *Extra,* the Sunday magazine of the *Baltimore News-American.* A graduate of the University of Maryland with a degree in journalism, Mr. Burdett completed graduate work at College Park in the American Civilization program. While in graduate school, his short story, "En Route" won a $100 prize in an international creative writing contest sponsored by *Writer's Digest* in which there were more than 25,000 entries.

Following graduate school, Mr. Burdett became news editor of the *Maryland Gazette,* oldest newspaper in continuous circulation in the United States. He was later drafted into the United States Army where he was assigned to the Public Information Office at Fort Lee, Virginia, and served as editor-in-chief of the *Fort Lee Traveller,* weekly newspaper of the United States Army's Quartermaster Training Command. He moonlighted in the Army as a sportswriter for the *Petersburg* (Va.) *Progress-Index* and as a disc jockey for Station WHAP in Hopewell, Virginia. From 1959 to 1962, he was a reporter for the *Baltimore News-American* covering state government and politics and writing a weekly political column. During the 1962 gubernatorial campaign, Mr. Burdett took a leave of absence from the *News-American* to manage the campaign of Democratic candidate David Hume. He returned to the *News-American* and remained for approximately one year before leaving to write a novel. In 1966, he joined the staff of the *Annapolis Evening Capital* as copy editor and political columnist.

Mr. Burdett became editorial page editor of the *Evening Capital* in 1968 and continued to write his political column. He was awarded first place in the Maryland-D.C.-Delaware Press Association editorial competition in 1966 for an editorial entitled "Requiem for a Patriot" recounting the story of the death of a young Annapolis soldier in a futile war in Southeast Asia. In 1970, Mr. Burdett won first place in the column competition of the Maryland-D.C.-Delaware Press Association. He is currently working on three books simultaneously—a book on contemporary Maryland politics scheduled for publication in 1975, the biography of a Maryland governor, and a political novel.

Mr. Burdett is a member of Sigma Delta Chi, the national journalism professional fraternity; Pi Delta Epsilon, the national journalism honorary (he served as president of his undergraduate chapter at the University of Maryland); the Maryland New Democratic Coalition; and the League of Women Voters. He was recently named to the Anne Arundel County Liaison Committee of the Maryland Historical Trust, and he holds membership in the Colonial Players of Annapolis and Historic Annapolis, Inc.

• • •

Eric Smith was born in Brooklyn, New York, in 1945, and now lives in Annapolis. He graduated from Georgetown University with a bachelor of arts in international affairs in 1967 and from the Georgetown Universtiy law school in 1972.

Mr. Smith served as an intelligence officer in Vietnam from 1967 until 1969; he was discharged with the rank of first lieutenant. He won second prize in the Maryland-D.C.-Delaware Press Association editorial cartoon competition in 1973, and serves as art director of *Maryland Free Lance,* a statewide political journal. He has been selected as one of the cartoonists whose work is appearing in the recently published *Best Editorial Cartoons of 1973.*

FOREWORD

At the outset the reader of these pages should be aware that it has not been the intention of the author to write the definitive history of Annapolis, or even to attempt another nondefinitive history of Annapolis. The former would be a worthwhile undertaking and we already have been deluged with the latter.

Although I had passed through Annapolis many times as a youngster, my real interest in the city did not begin until several years later when, as a political reporter for the *Baltimore News-American,* I became an annual "temporary" resident of the city during sessions of the Maryland General Assembly. The narrow, picturesque streets became a pleasant refuge from my observations of the lobbying, legislating and log-rolling that transpired within the walls of the venerable and historic State House.

Later I joined the staff of the *Evening Capital,* Annapolis' daily newspaper, and purchased a home in this city of unmatchable colonial charm. As a newsman my attention had been focused more on contemporaneous events than on the city's past. However, I was always distressed when a new ugliness marred this place that was very much becoming my home, and I always applauded intelligent efforts to preserve the elegant and charming colonial buildings and streets.

There is a definite fascination for me in being able to view daily any number of sights that the great and honored heroes of this nation's past—Washington, Jefferson, Franklin and so many others—once viewed; to walk the streets they walked and to understand their visions and aspirations for a young and struggling country.

As undeniably significant as are these physical reminders of our great heritage, a city such as Annapolis is much more than old brick and mortar. There are ghosts here, ghosts of giants who built this nation, others who were rascals and ruffians; but an overwhelming majority of those who created the atmosphere we call Annapolis were the plain and ordinary folk who just deemed themselves fortunate that they had found this quaint and lovely place in which to live.

The vignettes collected here were originally conceived as articles that were published in the *Evening Capital, Annapolitan Magazine* and *Extra,* the Sunday magazine of the *Baltimore News-American.* In writing these pieces, my hope was that the reader might gain a reasonable image of some of the inhabitants that once trod the streets of Annapolis—in my mind, if this could be successfully achieved it would serve to enhance one's appreciation of a truly remarkable little city. For the uniqueness of Annapolis is that it has fortunately retained sufficient visible evidence of its past so that the visitor, who is willing to use only a little imagination, can picture the street quarrel between the notorious Reverend Allen and the scion of the aristocratic Dulany family; the members of the Tuesday Club pompously marching to their meetings, each carrying his own individual spittoon as an emblem of mock honor; fiery Sam Chase convincing a street-corner gathering of the necessity of fighting to the death against British tyranny; the flashy Zouaves in their dazzling uniforms marching off to the dock to board ships that would take them to a battle most of them would never fight; and the gallant Spanish naval officers who were sent to Annapolis as prisoners of war but instead became ambassadors of good will.

It is a cliche to say that writing is one of the loneliest endeavors devised by man, and, along with most cliches, it also happens to be quite true. However, if I have succeeded in my purpose to portray some of those who once occupied the streets and homes of the city I cherish so deeply, I will have the satisfaction of feeling that in some small measure I have given back something to a city that has given me so much.

Harold N. Burdett

I

THE MAN WHO PUT ANNAPOLIS ON THE MAP

The name of Sir Francis Nicholson means little to the average Annapolitan today. But the spirited, adventurous, flamboyant and decisive Englishman is worthy of being honored as one who has perhaps done more for the City of Annapolis than anyone else in history. In fact, if it were not for Sir Francis, Annapolis might well have become a very different kind of town.

Nicholson served as Royal Governor of Maryland from 1694-1698. His name has been submerged in the city's past while patriots such as William Paca, Charles Carroll and Samuel Chase are more readily identified with the state capital.

But it was Sir Francis Nicholson who made the important decision to move the capital from St. Mary's City in Southern Maryland to Anne Arundel County. He also planned the town and selected the site on which the State House now stands.

It was Sir Francis Nicholson who proposed that a free school for boys be established in Annapolis; the result was the King William's School—forerunner of the present St. John's College.

And it was Sir Francis Nicholson who was responsible for erecting the first church on the city's picturesque Church Circle where St. Anne's Church now stands.

Sir Francis Nicholson can truly be considered the founder of Annapolis.

Before arriving in Maryland to succeed Sir Lionel Copley as Royal Governor, Nicholson had served as Deputy Governor of New York and Lieutenant Governor of Virginia. After leaving Maryland, he was named Royal Governor of Virginia, then Royal Governor of South Carolina, and, still later, Royal Governor of Nova Scotia.

One of Nicholson's more admirable qualities was his deep interest in education. This is reflected not only in his personal efforts toward founding King William's School, but also in the fact that he was responsible for establishing William and Mary College in Williamsburg, Virginia.

Shortly after he assumed his duties as Governor of the Colony of Maryland, Nicholson convened the assembly in Annapolis instead of its regular meeting place, St. Mary's City. And, at that session, Annapolis was made the permanent seat of government in the colony.

This was the realization of a dream for citizens of Annapolis, who for some two decades had been urging the assembly to move its activities to the city.

The reason behind Nicholson's decision to bring the capital to Annapolis had more to do with the political climate of the time than with his own personal feelings about the city.

King William, in order to strengthen his hold upon the colony, was anxious to placate the Protestants, who were in the majority in Maryland and who also happened to reside mainly on the banks of the Severn River. St. Mary's was a stronghold of Catholicism and the atmosphere there was charged with hostility towards the assembly which insisted upon popular government more than 80 years before the advent of the American Revolution.

However, it would be erroneous to conclude that Governor Nicholson was a mere sinecure of King William. The Governor possessed definite leadership qualities, and he was most eager to build a fitting capital city for the colony.

Nicholson went so far as to adopt principles of city planning. He reserved the highest elevation in Annapolis for public buildings (the area where the State House is now located). The land from the State House to the Severn River was set aside for the estates of the gentlemen of the community.

The western and southern portions of the city were earmarked for trade and industry—dyeing, tanning, brewing and baking. They were designated in spots where odors and eyesores would not offend the sensitivities of the local gentry.

Nicholson was also responsible for building the State House in Annapolis, a structure which was completed in 1697, only to burn down some seven years later.

A second State House was erected, but in 1772 it was replaced by the present building.

Historians have characterized Sir Francis Nicholson as a "passionate, high-handed . . . loose liver" with an "arrogant and overbearing temper."

A year after he departed from Annapolis to assume the governorship of Virginia, the then 44-year-old Nicholson became infatuated with 16-year-old Lucy Burwell of Gloucester County, Virginia. He wrote her a number of poems and love letters, many of which have been preserved in the Williamsburg archives.

A swaggering, swashbuckler, Governor Nicholson once took personal command of a ship and routed an entire fleet of pirates during an all-day battle on the Chesapeake Bay.

However, his jealous rage directed toward Edmund Berkeley, a tobacco planter who was also courting Miss Burwell, led to Nicholson's being recalled to England in 1705 by Queen Anne (for whom he had named Annapolis, which was originally called Anne Arundel Town).

All this notwithstanding, Annapolis owes much to Sir Francis Nicholson, whose basic concept for the city has not markedly changed during the last 280 years.

II

THE WOULD-BE BUCCANEER

The mere mention of piracy conjures up romantic legends of adventure on the high seas, Robert Louis Stevenson's immortal *Treasure Island,* the exploits of Captain Kidd, Blackbeard and Jean Lafitte, or Errol Flynn swashbuckling through his dashing roles of the 1930's and '40's. But no one remembers Richard Clarke of Annapolis.

Richard Clarke is probably forgotten because he never made it in the big leagues of buccaneering along with the more illustrious Kidd, Lafitte, Edward Teach and Henry Morgan. Since history does not record what finally became of Clarke, it is well within the realm of possibility that he never even got to raise the Jolly Roger.

If Clarke never succeeded in looting a hapless, unsuspecting vessel, if he never presided over the burial of heavy chests laden with jewels, silver and gold, it was not due to a lack of effort on his part. His maneuverings toward these goals did, after all, manage to cause quite a commotion among the members of the General Assembly of Maryland during the early years of the eighteenth century. Indignant citizens portrayed him as a maniacal villain whose insatiable appetite for treasure was rivaled only by his unquenchable thirst for alcohol.

It can be stated as a matter of uncontradictable fact that Richard Clarke was not a common criminal. To classify him as such would be to ignore both the magnitude of his conspiratorial plotting and the enormity of his talent for enlisting support in his questionable cause.

His alleged scheme to burn Annapolis (then the most important town in the entire province of Maryland) and simultaneously plunder the local arsenal, thoroughly and understandably enraged the colony's proprietary government back in 1707.

Clarke is described as "having a flat nose, peaked chinn and underjaw outsetting the upper." Thus, it is reasonable to assume that he did not rely upon a charismatic physical presence to attract his following. Chroniclers of the testimony in the case against Richard Clarke reported that greed motivated his co-conspirators, and that Clarke filled their pockets with counterfeit money he had the devious foresight to coin himself.

Addressing the House of Delegates in Annapolis on March 27, 1707, the Royal Governor, John Seymour, charged that august body with the investigation of allegations against Clarke in tones that had all the fine subtlety of an executioner sharpening a new axe. Governor Seymour's request to the legislators, in fact, sounded more like an indictment. He emphasized that the crimes of Richard Clarke were "so notoriously aggravated, they cry aloud for justice."

Four days later, a five-member committee of the General Assembly was selected to conduct the probe. And, on April 4, the House of Delegates issued a formal response to the Governor that clearly demonstrated its comprehension of the full impact of his message.

The House reply asserted that its membership was well aware of "Great and dangerous designs which have been carrying on by wicked people, enemys to Her Majestys Government, to destroy the records, arms and ammunition of this town, and all that was necessary to render this Government safe and secure...."

After profusely thanking the Governor for "the great care and prudence you have showed in the preservation of all those things, and the preventing (of) the effect of soe dangerous a conspiracy...," the House advised him to order the Attorney General to prosecute everyone found to be connected with the crimes.

The investigatory committee, headed by Colonel John Contee, went about the business of tracing the intricate web of conspiracy and reporting its findings to the House.

The committee concluded that Richard Clarke, Daniel Wells and "a certaine person who term'd himself a saylor" had plotted "to take some vessell, and get what assistance they could ... to disturb her Majestys peace and government, here, to make an attempt upon the Towne of Annapolis, and burn some houses here, and whilst that consternation continued, to seize the magazine and powder house to furnish themselves with arms and ammunition to goe a privateering...."

Furthermore, the committee ascertained that Clarke and his cohorts enticed "several housekeepers of desperate fortunes and other disaffected persons ... (and) several servants belonging to persons in and near the Towne of Annapolis and elsewhere to joine with them in their cursed and wicked designs and intent...."

The report goes on to tell of secret strategy meetings held in Annapolis and plans to steal either "Mr. Buff's boate" or "Mr. Evans Jones' Shallup" or "any other vessell fit for their turne, as soon as they had done their mischief here, to go to Carolina."

With the assistance of Daniel Wells and "the saylor," Clarke left Annapolis via the South River. Wells and the sailor returned to town to prepare the other conspirators; but, having spent some of the counterfeit money and fearing apprehension, they decided to follow Clarke after a meeting with William Simpson "at the House of Smithers in Annapolis."

Wells and the sailor made their way down the Chesapeake Bay. But five of the conspirators, including Simpson, whom the committee felt was a leading figure in the scheme, were caught and sent to prison.

The report of the committee said that Wells and the seaman, following Clarke, came to Long Island in the Bay where Clarke had been the day before. Armed with powder and shot and sailing a small boat, the two conspirators posed as deputies under orders of the High Sheriff of Anne Arundel County to pursue Clarke. Meanwhile, the committee concluded, Clarke had settled in News River in Carolina pretending to be a merchant and attempting to persuade the inhabitants to join him.

The House concurred in the committee's report and both Houses passed a bill for the attainder of Clarke on April 9. But this did not end the investigation of the conspiracy which, if carried out, could have dealt a severely damaging blow to the entire province as well as the town of Annapolis.

Captain Sylvester Welch was called before the Governor's Council to answer a charge of selling "the country's powder" to Clarke's accomplices. Welch admitted selling powder to them, but he insisted he sold only what belonged to him; he contended that what remained of three pounds of the country's powder left in his charge could be found at his house, but that he had fired away the rest during the previous summer. Refusing to believe Welch, Governor Seymour promptly discharged the captain from his command.

Meanwhile, the High Sheriff of Anne Arundel County, Major Josiah Wilson, arrested John Spry, skipper of the sloop *Margaret's Industry,* and Thomas Brereton, who had recently arrived at South River from Virginia. While neither was willing to confess to complicity in Clarke's scheme, it was subsequently learned by the Council "that Clarke haunts . . . the Rosey Crowne in Norfolk Towne."

Eventually Spry and Brereton admitted that Clarke had sent them after his wife, children and household goods and that they also delivered a letter from Clarke to Joseph Hill, a member of the House of Delegates, who had given them assistance.

Hill was arrested and on April 10 was brought before the Council where the depositions of Spry and Brereton were read to him. Hill claimed he had not seen Clarke in the past year and did not have the foggiest notion of his whereabouts. The delegate also denied receiving a letter from Clarke, but Spry and Brereton were brought in and both identified Hill as the one to whom they had taken the letter.

On the following day, Hill was expelled from the House "till he be cleared of what is lay'd to his charge."

The act of attainder against Clarke, which said he "had obstinately refused to surrender himself to justice," was not his first brush with the law. Similar charges had been placed against him two years earlier.

There is no evidence in the court records of Anne Arundel County as to what, if any, punishment came to Richard Clarke and his henchmen. It has been theorized that Clarke was never captured, but it is still unclear whether or not he got very far with his "great and dangerous designs."

We may assume that the uncharacteristic haste of the legislature to uncover the Clarke conspiracy very probably saved some boats from being stolen and some Annapolis homes from being burned. But Clarke, the would-be buccaneer of old Annapolis, remains an intriguing mystery man of the city's past.

The Tuesday Club

III

THE TUESDAY CLUB

The development of conversation into something of an art came about almost as a matter of necessity in Annapolis during the middle years of the eighteenth century. The town was already beginning to be recognized as a major cultural center of the colonies and it was unquestionably the most important city in the province of Maryland. The town's racetrack, theater and lavish balls and dinners were to draw visitors from far and wide. But in a day when there were no television sets to huddle around and stifle verbal exchange, men of intelligence, culture and wit sought each other out for fellowship. This led to the emergence of clubs designed to showcase the storytelling abilities of the members. The club phenomenon in Annapolis owes much to Dr. Alexander Hamilton.

In the year 1739, Dr. Hamilton, a native of Edinburgh, Scotland, settled in Annapolis, where there was a need for a competent physician, and he soon built a large and lucrative practice. One probable reason for his immediate success might have been one of his favorite remedies, illustrated by the following exchange between the physician and the young painter, Charles Willson Peale:

"What is the best drink for health?" asked Peale.

"Toddy, mun," replied Hamilton. "The spirit must hae something to act on, and therefore acts on the sugar and does nae injury to the stomach."

It is apparent that Hamilton established his reputation for a comic spirit during his early years in Scotland from this line in a letter written from home by his sister: "Alas! how much scotch drollery is now transplanted into American soil."

Dr. Hamilton had been in Annapolis for only a very short time before he began suffering from the oppressive summer weather; he seriously considered returning to the British Isles where he felt the climate was more agreeable.

"I am not well in health," he wrote a friend in Scotland in November, 1743, "and for that reason chiefly I continue Still a Batchellor." From his description of his illness, it seems almost certain he had contracted tuberculosis.

The following year, Dr. Hamilton, accompanied by his black slave, Dromo, journeyed by horseback and sloop as far as Portsmouth, New Hampshire, and wrote a daily journal in which he recorded his impressions of places he visited and persons he met.

In 1745 he conceived the idea of forming the Tuesday Club. The first meeting was held in his home on May 14th. The idea came from the Whin-Brush Club to which he belonged in Edinburgh and which met every Friday evening for the purpose of drinking "two penny ale," smoking tobacco and the amusement of members.

Most of what is known about the Tuesday Club is derived from an entertaining three-volume history of the club penned by Dr. Hamilton. But because of Hamilton's tongue-in-cheek style it is sometimes difficult to discern between his descriptions of actual club meetings and "events" that are total products of his formidable imagination.

The "Ancient and Honourable Tuesday Club," wrote Dr. Hamilton, was "designed for humor . . . a sort of farcical Drama of Mock Majesty" which assembled weekly at the home of a "long-standing member."

Furthermore, Dr. Hamilton is insistent that there were "forerunners" of the Tuesday Club in Annapolis, and that among these were the Royalist, Redhouse and Ugly clubs. However, it is highly questionable that any of the three latter clubs ever existed; more probably, they were invented as a facetious effort by Hamilton to "explain" the origin of the Tuesday Club. In his account, Dr. Hamilton claims that one George Neilson was the founder of the Royalist and Redhouse clubs. George Neilson was not a fictitious person; he was among a number of Scottish political prisoners sent to Maryland in 1716, and he is known to have remained in Annapolis to ply his trade of silversmith.

The tone of the club's history, dated from Hamilton's study on September 9, 1754, is immediately established in the dedication to "the venerable chancellor of the ancient and honourable Tuesday Club and his successor in that honourable office"; it goes on to express the amusing opinion that dedications are "at best but paltry stuff" in which truth is warped "either by the power of flattery or by the pestilent inclination to party, or pusillanimous fear of the anger and resentment of men in power."

The club had many of the trappings of later fraternal organizations including a secret handshake, metal badges worn only on ceremonial occasions, the practice of raising a large canopy in the shape of a scallop shell and ornamented with the club's motto and shield above the president's chair (which was designed so that it was several inches higher than the chairs of other members), an annual ball to honor the ladies, and a collection of sixpence from each member at every meeting for the club's charitable fund.

Hamilton's mock history includes lengthy recitations of the club odes, acrostics, conundrums, puns, anniversary poems, speeches, music and songs. The text is adorned by grotesque India ink caricatures of members and riotous sketches of club meetings.

Members were given special club names. Club president Charles Cole was referred to as the Right Honorable Master Jole, Esq.; William Thornton, renowned for his singing voice, was dubbed Protomusicus;

Dr. Hamilton was known as Loquacious Scribble, Esq. Other pseudonyms included: Huffman Snap, Esq.; Solo Neverout, Esq.; Quirpum Comic, Esq.; Jonathan Grog, Esq., and the sergeant-at-arms and high steward acquired the tag of Prim Timorous, Esq.

When William Thornton was honored as chief musician, a rule was passed requiring him "to sing his vote in a musical manner else it is to go for nothing." Thornton was also extended the privilege of commanding any member of the group to sing after rendering a song himself.

At one meeting, Thornton was accused of negligence in office, but the club president decided against punitive action; as a demonstration of gratitude, Thornton sang two songs.

Music played a considerable role in the activities of the Tuesday Club, for, in addition to frequent outbursts of song from Thornton and other members, Dr. Hamilton tells us that the Reverend Thomas Bacon, the first scholar to undertake the Herculean task of compiling the laws of Maryland, was made an honorary member because of his accomplishments as a fiddler. Dr. Hamilton critiqued Bacon's performance by saying that he "played agreeable on the violin."

Another parson provided musical accompaniment for dancing. The minutes of one meeting note: "Before the club broke up, the Rev. Mr. Howard played several jigs, hornpipes and minuets solo to which Sir John, champion knight of the club, danced several bold and warlike dances."

A delightful club rule was the so-called "gelastic law" whereby any member who mentioned religion or politics would be laughed at until he dropped the subject. There is an account of Protomusicus Thornton breaking the rule and "the whole company being seized with a most vociferous and roaring laugh, which Mr. Protomusicus himself joined, with most prodigious force of lungs."

Jonas Green, printer and publisher of the *Maryland Gazette* and one of Dr. Hamilton's closest friends, was inducted into the club in 1748 and delivered the following speech:

"I have the best reasons in the world to be satisfied with this good society, as I find everything in it that is sociable and agreeable, and besides, I find we eat and drink well, hence must flow good humor, and as a consequence of this we must sleep well—and the society seems to be settled on so firm a basis, that nothing but death can separate the members of it one from another...."

He concluded with: "May good fellowship dispel every cloud that may threaten us, excepting on that of tobacco, the dear specific condensator of political conceptions."

Indeed, the inseparable comradeship of club members is borne out in a letter written by one club member, Stephen Bordley, to another, Witham Marshe (then visiting in England). Informing Marshe of Dr.

Hamilton's marriage to Miss Margaret Dulany, daughter of the wealthy Daniel Dulany, Bordley writes that "poor Hamilton is gone—not dead, but married. He was the day before yesterday obliged to throw himself up to the Mony of Peggy Dulany, and is already what you would from your knowledge of this Lady now suppose him to be, a very Grave sober fellow."

How "grave" and "sober" Hamilton had become after his marriage is certainly open to debate since his rollicking mock history of the club was written seven years after his wedding ceremony. It is also true that the Tuesday Club flourished mainly due to the doctor's efforts, until he died in 1764.

However, there is evidence that even though the Tuesday Club's first toast of the evening was always in honor of the ladies (the second toast was to "the King's Majesty" and the third to "the Deluge"), the women did not always appreciate the club's activities. On one occasion, Hamilton left the Minute Book—in which he recorded the proceedings of each meeting—on a table and stepped out of the room. He returned later to find some of the members' wives busily deleting certain passages of which they did not approve.

The practice of club members carrying their own individual sandbox spittoons to meetings was abandoned after a while. Hamilton explained that the use of the sandboxes "was fallen upon to prevent abusing and soiling the floors of the rooms where the club sat; and these conveniences were carried about with great pomp and solemnity from one Steward's house to another, every time the club met; but cleanly and useful as they were and contrived for the ease of servants and neat housewives, whose chief ambition and care of life is to make their plank floors shine like glass, yet, they were dismissed, because it was thought that the married men of the club were afraid of falling under the ridicule of the bachelors by showing in this, a more common care and solicitude about incurring the displeasures of their wives."

A proposal came before the club to disqualify bachelors from future membership, but Hamilton records that "this inhuman act was not passed, to their credit be it spoken. We all know that that respectable although unfortunate class of men constitute the most useful members of some societies with which we are familiar. But I presume the main reason in this case was that bachelors, usually not being housekeepers, could not entertain the club, but that reason does not apply to some bachelors of our acquaintance, who, some of us present can testify with most appetizing recollections, entertain more sumptuously than the Benedicts."

When the Tuesday Club was first organized, a schedule was drawn up so that at each meeting at least one member would speak on a topic of his own choice. Among the topics were charity, cheerfulness, wisdom and clubs. But the formal programs were eventually dropped, the members preferring the spontaneous give-and-take of impromptu discussions and arguments.

The members, comprised mainly of planters and professional men, sat around the fireplace smoking their clay pipes, drinking Jamaica rum and telling jokes and riddles; the circumspect Jonas Green distinguished himself in these sessions as a spinner of risqué yarns. But Green was much more than a raconteur. He was designated as P.P.P.P.P. (poet, printer, punster, purveyor and punchmaker), doubtless the most versatile member of the Tuesday Club.

As a sample of his poetic talent, we have Green's toast to President Cole (Jole):

> Wishing this ancient club may always be
> Promoters of facetious mirth and glee,
> And that our members all may be expert
> At the great punning and conundrum art,
> And that our Laureate's muse may ever warble,
> Our fame to last as grav'd on brass or marble,
> And while gay laughter furbishes each soul,
> Let each a bumper drink to noble Jole.

One favorite pastime of the club was to hold mock trials of culprits who had violated the club constitution or had not treated President Cole with proper respect. Indicted on a nonsensical charge, Jonas Green was taken into custody by the sergeant-at-arms "and he was confined for a full half hour a languishing prisoner in a remote corner of the room being deprived of all comfort and assistance from the sparkling and enlivening board—a woeful and lamentable spectacle, and a warning to all loyal members to be upon their good behaviour."

The membership admired one of Green's poems to the point of ordering its London plenipotentiary, Anthony Bacon, to have the composition inserted in a London literary magazine. However, when he approached the publisher of the *Universal Magazine* with Green's effort, Bacon was told that the author was a fool.

Hamilton read Bacon's letter describing the scene at a meeting of the club. When Hamilton was finished reading, the rejected author rose and said it was fortunate the poem was turned down because Colley Cibber, Green's successor as poet laureate, might have done to him what Pope did to Edmund Curll, the London stationer: "That is, have poisoned me under the mask of friendship with a glass of old hock as a whet before dinner, knowing I am naturally fond of whets."

Among the first laws of the Tuesday Club was that "the member appointed to serve as steward, shall provide a gammon of bacon, or any other dish of vittels and no more." Later, for some obscure reason, it was ordained that "such as are bachelor members, may be permitted to have cheese instead of dressed vittels." And still later, Hamilton reported: "Resolved that cheese is not any more to be deemed a dish of vittels and therefore the use of it as such in this here club is forbid."

Liquor flowed freely at the meetings, but there was a strict rule that "no fresh liquor shall be made, prepared or produced after 11 o'clock at night." Furthermore, any member who lingered on at the steward's house after the 11 o'clock adjournment hour could be fined one shilling. These provisions were doubtless in deference to the wives and families of members who were married.

Hamilton gives this account of a typical meeting of the club:

> The candles being lit, the punch made and the pipes fairly set going, after 2 or 3 rounds of the punch bowl, they applied themselves to make and to pass some wholesome laws for the good government and regulation of the Society.... Having passed these laws with great wisdom and sagacity, they betook themselves again to their punch and pipes and then the gammon, according to rule, appeared on the sideboard, with some plates in a heap and knives and forks, there not being so much as the formality of a cloth laid and every member at pleasure arose from his seat and helped himself, without taking up time in saying grace, setting chairs, passing compliments, about taking place at table or troubling themselves about shifting of dishes, handling of plates, spoons, cruets, mustard pots, etc., and servants running over one another which not only wastes much time but creates more noise than is needful.

One of the club members was indicted for holding back nine bottles of English beer which had been presented to him for the club's use. He was tried and found innocent of the charge of converting the beer to his own use. However, he was found guilty of reclaiming the gift beer in his own hands for his service night; he was "gently censured" for this crime.

Another member was indicted because he, "in the presence of several members of this club, with force and arms, wickedly, made an open assault upon the chair, honor and person of the President, in open contempt of the laws of this club, then and there, taking into your hands a certain punch bowl of the value of 4 s. and most impudently, audaciously and insolently, the punch bowl, charged with a certain liquor called Punch, to your mouth uplifting, drank the first toast after supper against an express law of the Club."

President Cole suffered from the gout and he frequently was unable to attend meetings. On these occasions, Cole instructed Hamilton to draw up a letter of appointment in which he designated a member to chair the meeting in his absence. Because Cole was absent so often, Hamilton became weary of the task of making out so many certificates and the physician settled the matter by convincing Jonas Green to print a form that would serve the purpose.

When Cole recovered from his illness, he was honored by a Jonas

Green poem bearing the windy title of: "A congratulatory Pindaric Ode, addressed to the Right Honorable Master Jole, Esq., President of the ancient and honorable Tuesday Club, on his having escaped the cruel distemper of the gout, this present year 1755, by his most obedient and very humble servant the club's Poet Laureate." The poem was set down as follows:

>Descend, ye muses from Parnassus hill,
>And drop nepenthe in my raptur'd quill,
>>High, O High,
>
>Let my tow'ring genius fly!
>And in ecstatic numbers sing our joy,
>Not only that great Jole's alive,
>In seventeen hundred fifty five,
>But now, that hoary winter fast retreats
>And turns his back on spring's mild genial heats,
>>And yet great Jole is found
>>Vigorous, brisk, and sound,
>
>Nor is one precious joint possess'd
>With that worst curst tormenting pest,
>>The gout, the raging gout,
>
>Kind Heaven at last has from his limbs kept out,
>>And we, with joy again,
>>Released from racking pain,
>
>Now see him mount the chair
>With firm and vigorous tread,
>And sound, judicious head,
>The club as he was wont to regulate,
>Each law he dictates, tempers each debate,
>Obedience to enforce, he sagely plies his cane.

Tuesday Club members constantly battled to limit the constitutional powers of their president. But it is obvious they held him in high esteem. In 1752, they asked the portrait painter, Mr. Hesselius (probably John, son of Gustav Hesselius), to paint a full-length portrait of Charles Cole. Cole died in 1757, leaving an amount of personal property valued at less than 200 pounds; he owed money to Benjamin Tasker and Daniel Dulany, two of Annapolis' wealthiest citizens and landowners of that era.

The membership of the club included several lawyers—among them, Stephen Bordley, John Beale Bordley, William Cumming and James Calder—and planters, including James Hollyday, William Rogers and Edward Dorsey. The Reverend John Gordon, rector of St. Anne's parish from 1745-1749, attended nearly every meeting during those years.

The wealthiest man connected with the club was Hamilton's father-in-law, Daniel Dulany, but wealth was certainly not a prerequisite for membership. In fact, the only person on record who was blackballed by the Tuesday Club, was John Raitt, an Annapolis merchant whose property was worth over 2,500 pounds. Raitt was nominated by Dr. Hamilton, but several members voted him down.

The Tuesday Club seems to have dissolved around the time of the death of Hamilton, its founder and guiding spirit, in 1764. However, other clubs emerged in Annapolis, the foremost of which was the Homony Club, which was organized in 1770 and met at the Coffee House, one of the chief taverns in the town.

Those desiring membership in the Homony Club were required to submit an application in the form of a humorous poetic epistle full of puns; thus, there was a high premium on literary ability. Many of Annapolis' most distinguished citizens were members of the Homony Club, including William Eddis, author of *Letters from America;* the Reverend Jonathan Boucher, outspoken Tory rector of St. Anne's and tutor of George Washington's stepson; Charles Willson Peale, artist and painter of Washington, and William Paca, signer of the Declaration of Independence.

This account of the history and origin of the Homony Club is contained in the reminiscences of the Reverend Boucher:

> Three or four social and literary men proposed the institution of a weekly club under the title of The Homony Club, of which I was the first president. It was, in fact, the best club in all respects I have ever heard of, as the sole object of it was to promote innocent mirth and ingenious humor. We had a secretary, and books in which all our proceedings were recorded; and as every member conceived himself bound to contribute some composition, either in verse or prose, and we had also many mirthfully ingenious debates, our archives soon swelled to two or three folios, replete with much miscellaneous wit and fun.
>
> I had a great share in its proceedings, and it soon grew into such fame that the Governor and all the principal people of the country ambitiously solicited the honor of being members or honorary visitants. It lasted as long as I stayed in Annapolis, and was finally broken up only when the troubles began and put an end to everything that was pleasant and proper.

The "troubles" of which Boucher spoke were the results of growing political bitterness that presaged the Revolutionary War, making it increasingly less possible for a William Paca and a Jonathan Boucher to share in the promotion of "innocent mirth and ingenious humor."

IV

THE UNPRINCIPLED PARSON

When the Reverend Bennet Allen arrived in Annapolis from England in 1767 to become pastor of St. Anne's Church, the parishioners saw a handsome, cultured clergyman with an ample gift of eloquence. What they failed to recognize immediately was his marked propensity for venality and violence, characteristics that would make him one of the most despised men in the colony of Maryland.

A graduate of Wadham College, Oxford, Allen came to Anne Arundel County as a minister more interested in seeking wealth than saving souls. He brought with him a letter from Lord Baltimore who spoke of his "great personal regard and friendship" for Allen and instructed the proprietary governor, Horatio Sharpe, to see that the clergyman "shall have one of the best livings" that could be offered in the entire province.

On April 20, 1767, the Reverend Allen became rector of St. Anne's parish. He was most favorably received and, indeed, he spent his first year's income to improve the property of the church.

Six months later, Governor Sharpe, heeding his orders from Lord Baltimore, also gave the minister a license as the curate of St. James' parish at Herring Bay, 16 miles south of Annapolis. This led to a thorny question as to whether a clergyman should be able to hold two parishes at the same time. Insisting on holding both parishes, Allen cited Lord Baltimore's instructions that he be given two livings if no single parish afforded adequate support. Allen also called attention to the law that made plural benefices legal, provided that the vestries of both agreed to the arrangement.

The parson set forth on January 6, 1768, to take possession of St. James'. On his way he stopped at the home of Samuel Chew, a St. James' vestryman who supported his intentions.

While Chew was preparing a bowl of punch to refresh his visitor, Allen informed him that he planned to rent the property of the church. Chew told him he had no right to do this and pointed to the Acts of Assembly in an effort to support his argument.

The Reverend Allen replied, "You don't consider the spirit of the law."

"You don't consider your own interest and the spirit of the devil perhaps," fumed the vestryman.

Allen expressed surprise to discover that so many men learned in the law could not construe the "spirit of the law." He further accused Chew of going against his word to vote for Allen's holding of two parishes.

Acknowledging that he had promised his support, Chew said he had reconsidered the propriety of the situation and had changed his mind. When the minister harped on the vestryman's promise, Chew said he was standing fast and that he had already been ridiculed for his original decision to back the minister.

"My friend," Allen said, "you shan't be blamed about it. I'll take the burden off your shoulders."

Chew angrily arose and started to leave the room, but he remained when the clergyman again mentioned his pledge and told him he was expecting letters from England that would resolve the matter once and for all. Allen then paused and said, "I know where this sudden change comes from: Ay, Dulany! Dulany!"

Allen was clearly paranoid about Daniel Dulany, one of Annapolis' most esteemed citizens at the time, who vociferously contended that the Maryland Established Church was a weak, corrupt and prostituted institution—the embodiment of injustice and falsehood.

Startled by Allen's outburst, Chew contended: "Sir, you have no right to reflect on any gentleman, for I give you my word and honor, I have had no conversation with Mr. Dulany, nor know his sentiments on it."

After the minister repeated several times that he doubted Chew's veracity, the vestryman found a Bible on a nearby desk and, placing his hand upon it, said:

"Sir, I can here solemnly swear that I have had no conversation with Mr. Dulany, nor know anything of his being your enemy in it, than you have told me yourself."

"Notwithstanding that, sir," replied the clergyman, "I should much doubt or question your word."

Outraged by Allen's audacity, Chew seized him by the collar and threw him out of the house, advising him to: "Go and learn better manners before you come to a gentleman's home again."

The clergyman subsequently challenged Chew to a duel and the vestryman accepted on the condition that the two men would meet alone. The duel did not materialize. On the appointed day, Chew arrived on the field of honor with a servant who was armed with a blunderbuss. But he received a note from Allen calling off the meeting because of inclement weather and the "informality" of the arrangements.

Allen's fight with Chew was not the only occasion upon which his conduct precipitated the exchange of blows while he was in Anne Arundel County. The minister became involved in a quarrel on the streets of Annapolis with Walter Dulany, the son of Daniel Dulany. Walter Dulany, who was described as a "heavy, gouty and clumsy man," managed to take the minister's sword cane away from him and, before a crowd that had quickly gathered, severely thrashed Allen with it. The clergyman stripped off his coat and shouted, "By God, I will box you."

Allen might have come off with something worse than a caning had his sister not intruded and dragged him away from the scene. This same sister was once called in a letter written by the Reverend Jonathan Boucher, who later succeeded Allen as rector of St. Anne's, "a Sister to him as Sarah was to Abraham."

A few days later Allen again encountered Dulany on the streets of Annapolis and attacked him impulsively. But Allen eventually expressed a desire to forgive and forget the quarrel. Two years after the caning, Dulany accused the parson of attempting to bribe an indentured servant to assassinate him. Defending himself, Allen insisted that to trust a recently purchased indentured servant with such an errand would have been "Folly, or rather Madness." The minister expounded the theory that the servant had told Dulany the tale in an effort to gain his freedom, but the accusation was considered sufficiently serious for the parson to appear before the Provincial Court to answer it.

Still mindful of the letter of instruction from Lord Baltimore and most probably due to the animosity Allen had created in Anne Arundel County, Governor Sharpe presented the clergyman with the vacated All Saints Parish in Frederick—one of the wealthiest in the entire colony.

When the minister arrived in Frederick, he found a solid block of opposition to his taking over the parish. Again Allen blamed Dulany for his troubles, but he obtained the keys and gained entrance to the church. Later, parishioners removed the locks from the doors and bolted them from the inside. But on Sunday, Allen, using a ladder, climbed into a window of the church and unbolted the doors.

The vestry approached the minister and declared he was guilty of a breach of privilege, to which he replied: "I am not acquainted with the customs. The moment the Governor signs an induction, your power ceases. . . ."

When the vestry retreated to the doors of the church, Allen went to the pulpit, apologized to the congregation for the delay and began his service. The vestry summoned the parishioners out of the church and the minister continued with the service as though nothing had happened. Then, according to Allen's personal account of the fiasco, "I heard some commotion from without which gave me alarm, and I provided, luckily, against it, or I must have been maimed if not murdered."

Some of the largest men among the congregation reentered the church, appearing intent upon pulling him from the pulpit.

"I let the captain come within two paces of me, and clapt my pistol to his head," Allen wrote in a letter describing the bizarre episode to Governor Sharpe. "What consternation! They accuse me of swearing by God, I would shoot him; I believe I did swear, which was better than praying just then."

At the sight of the minister's pistol, the vestry retreated. Allen proceeded with the service until the doors and windows flew open and stones were hurled into the church. Allen said his aide-de-camp, Mr. Dakein, advised him to leave the church, and, "We walked through the midst of them, facing about from time to time, till we got some distance when stones began to fly. I luckily escaped any hurt and Dakein had but one blow."

Leaving a respected vestryman in charge of the parish, Allen went to Philadelphia where he published an article in the *Pennsylvania Chronicle* accusing the Dulanys of inciting the Frederick mob and of trying to wrest the government of Maryland from Lord Baltimore's hands.

Allen returned to England where he published another attack on the Dulany family in the *London Evening Post* of January 29, 1779. Entitled "Characters of the Principal Men of the Rebellion," the article accused the Dulanys of playing both sides during the Revolution; it claimed that while part of the family fled to England, Daniel Dulany was staying behind in Maryland to save the family property no matter which side won. The same article described George Washington as nothing more than a land speculator whose "abilities are of that mediocrity which created no jealousy" and criticized the private life of Benjamin Franklin and expressed the hope that "if the axe or the haltar are to be employed on this occasion . . . the first example could be made of this hoary traitor."

Lloyd Dulany, who was in England at the time, succeeded in having the *Post* withdraw the charges two days after they appeared in the newspaper. Dulany also challenged the anonymous author of the article.

For three years, Allen did not openly admit authorship of the article and he avoided any encounters with the Dulanys. However, Allen and Lloyd Dulany accidentally met near Hyde Park in June of 1782 and Dulany challenged him to a duel. After procuring ammunition for Allen's pistols, they drove through the gates of the park at early twilight. Lloyd Dulany insisted it was not dark enough to prevent the duel. They fired at a distance of eight yards and Lloyd fell from a shot through the lung. He was taken to his house on Park Street where he died three days later.

Allen was tried on a charge of manslaughter, found guilty and fined one shilling and sentenced to six months' imprisonment. Although it is not certain what became of Allen, the minister who once said that his income at St. Anne's was hardly sufficient to keep him in liquor, and another time said, "I am not happy enough to live without wine," reportedly wandered the streets of London as a degenerate drunkard and died in wretched poverty.

V

THE CRITICAL CLERGYMAN

George Washington's most memorable visit to Annapolis was when he came to resign his commission in the Continental Army at the State House on December 23, 1783. But on that significant occasion, General Washington was already well acquainted with the city.

Prior to the Revolution, Annapolis was a major social center of the colonies, and Washington, a man of great wealth and social standing, made frequent trips from Virginia to attend the races, the theater and the balls and dinners.

However, he had another more personal reason for maintaining a deep interest in the city; for it was to Annapolis that he sent his stepson, John Parke Custis, to receive his education under the tutelage of the Reverend Jonathan Boucher, rector of St. Anne's parish from 1770 to 1772.

Educated in the divinity and ordained in England, Boucher returned to Virginia, where he had earlier made his living as a tutor, and began serving as a minister. In addition, he conducted a school for boys and young Custis was one of his pupils. When Boucher secured a parish in Annapolis, Washington sent Master Custis to continue his education with the clergyman.

However, Boucher seems to have had his hands full in managing both the more demanding obligations of a larger parish and the teaching of a group of several young boys. Washington, who was conscientiously concerned by the boy's lack of progress in Annapolis, frequently corresponded with the clergyman about this situation.

In one of these letters, dated December 16, 1770, Washington lamented the fact that Jacky Custis seemed more interested in dogs, horses and guns than in his studies. Moreover, Washington pleaded with Boucher to keep a close watch on the 15-year-old boy, who was now advancing into a time of life that would require "the most friendly aid and counsel (especially in such a place as Annapolis)...."

Washington said "the warmth of (young Custis') own passions, assisted by the bad example of other youth, may prompt him to actions derogatory of virtue...." The future first President of the United States said he definitely did not want his stepson "to be rambling about of nights in the company with those who do not care how debauched and vicious his conduct may be."

Boucher's difficulty in coping with Master Custis was expressed when he wrote Washington: "I never did in my life know a youth so exceedingly indolent, or so surprisingly voluptuous; one would suppose nature had intended him for some Asiatic prince."

The clergyman informed Washington that the boy received many invitations to visits, balls and "other scenes of pleasure" but "seldom or never goes . . . without learning something I could have wished him not to have learned."

And Boucher added: "There are not, that I know of, more idle or pleasurable people in Annapolis than there are in any other town containing an equal number of inhabitants: yet somehow or other he (Custis) has contrived to learn a great deal of idleness and dissipation among them. One inspires him with a passion for dress—another for racing, fox-hunting, etc. . . ."

Boucher eventually left St. Anne's and Custis was later sent to King's College in New York, but three months later the young man returned to Mount Vernon where, at the age of 19, he married 16-year-old Eleanor Calvert. Custis and Miss Calvert had become engaged, without the consent of either of their families, while he was studying in Annapolis. The marriage seems to have been a happy one until Custis, while serving as Washington's aide-de-camp, died during the Yorktown campaign.

While he was in Annapolis, the Reverend Boucher's rabid Tory sentiments caused him to be brought before the patriot committee. According to his own account, he managed to charm the members of the committee with his eloquence. However, during his last six months as a minister in Maryland he always went to the pulpit with a pair of loaded pistols.

The minister, who later wrote of Annapolis as being "the genteelest town in North America" and that he hardly knew "a town in England so desirable to live in as Annapolis was then," proved not nearly as generous in his appraisal of General Washington.

Of Washington, Boucher said he could not conceive "how he could, otherwise than through the interested representations of party, have ever been spoken of as a great man. He is shy, silent, stern, slow and cautious; but has no quickness of parts, extraordinary penetration, nor an elevated style of thinking."

While characterizing Washington as "regular, temperate, strictly just and honest," Boucher concludes: "But he seems to have nothing generous or affectionate in his nature. Just before the close of the last war he married the widow Custis, and thus came into the possession of her large jointure. He never had any children, and lived very much like a gentleman at Mount Vernon, in Fairfax County, where the most distinguished part of his character was that he was an admirable farmer."

VI

SON OF DISCORD

Samuel Chase's Tory enemies in Annapolis called him "Bacon Face," no doubt because of his florid complexion that suggested he was an excessive imbiber.

But this lawyer-patriot and signer of the Declaration of American Independence was called much worse.

In fact, the conservative mayor and aldermen of Annapolis proclaimed him a "busy, restless incendiary, a ringleader of mobs, a foul-mouthed and inflaming son of discord and faction, a common disturber of the public tranquility, and a promoter of the lawless excesses of the multitudes."

The description had the clear ring of truth. But Chase was not one to shrink from such a challenge; among the milder invectives he unleashed upon his critics was that they were "despicable tools of power, emerged from obscurity and basking in proprietary sunshine."

Sam Chase did not limit his talent for rebelliousness to name-calling. He was a vigorous activist who did much to spread the spirit of the American Revolution throughout Maryland and when the colonies sent their representatives to Philadelphia to decide upon a course of action, his was one of the more hawkish voices.

Tutored by his father, the Reverend Thomas Chase, who was a scholar of Hebrew and Latin in England before settling in Baltimore, the 18-year-old Samuel had the equivalent of a college education in the classics when he arrived in Annapolis in 1759 to study law in the offices of John Hammond and John Hall.

Within five years, he became a member of the Maryland General Assembly where he promptly joined the opposition to the royal governor and supported such measures as regulating clerical salaries which cut his own father's salary in half.

He also aligned himself with the extremist Sons of Liberty, whose violent reactions to the British Parliament's Stamp Act of 1765 were responsible for arousing the wrath of the Annapolis city fathers. When Parliament later repealed the Stamp Act, Chase addressed these words to his fellow colonists:

"I admit, gentlemen, that I was one of those committed to the flames, in effigy, the stamp distributor of this province, and who openly disputed the parliamentary right to tax the colonies, while you skulked in your houses, some of you asserting the parliamentary right, and esteeming the Stamp Act as a beneficial law. Others of you meanly grumbled in your corners, not daring to speak out your sentiments."

Chase continued to voice his opposition to the tyranny of Great Britain and in 1774 he became a member of the Maryland Committee of Correspondence and a delegate to the First Continental Congress. He was extremely dissatisfied when that august body decided to seek peaceful solutions to the grievances with England.

Long before the colonists decided to take up arms, he was making radical speeches declaring that he "owed no allegiance to the King of Great Britain." Such sentiments invariably flustered his more conservative colleagues.

The meeting of the Continental Congress in 1775, after fighting had begun at Lexington and Concord, was more to his liking. There he urged a total embargo on trade with Great Britain, which he contended would speedily force the oppressors into submission or bankruptcy. Voting for the organization of the Continental Army, he was a leading supporter of appointing George Washington as its commander-in-chief.

Chase won the admiration of the Continental Congress when he took the floor to fearlessly expose one of its members, John Joachim Zubly, a Presbyterian clergyman, as a traitor. The Marylander learned that Zubly had been writing to the royal governor of Georgia about the Congress' consideration of independence for the colonies. Zubly managed to escape to Georgia where he was protected by the proprietary governor.

In 1776, Chase accompanied Charles Carroll, Benjamin Franklin and John Carroll on an unsuccessful mission aimed at enlisting the support of Canada on the side of the American colonists against Great Britain. When he returned to Philadelphia in June, Chase discovered that the instructions of Maryland delegates to Congress prevented them from voting for independence.

He hastened to Maryland where he stumped extensively before gatherings of farmers and villagers, imploring them to let the Legislature know that they wanted the instructions changed. His efforts succeeded and he returned to Philadelphia in time to sign the Declaration of Independence on July 4th.

Chase continued to serve in Congress until 1778 when it was discovered that he had used inside information obtained as a member of Congress to make a profit on the sale of flour to the army.

He returned to Annapolis where he continued to serve in the Maryland Legislature and practice law. Once on a trip to Baltimore, he attended a meeting of a local debating society where he was impressed with the oratorical skills of a young apprentice pharmacist. Learning that the young man had no funds to pay for his law studies, Chase brought him to Annapolis to study law under his personal guidance. The young man, William Pinkney, later served as a diplomat, a United States Senator and Attorney General of the United States.

Chase, whose first wife, Anne Baldwin of Annapolis, died in 1778 after 16 years of marriage, met and married Hannah Kitty Giles while on a mission to London in 1784. He failed, however, at the original purpose of the trip which was to recover some $800,000 owed to the colony of Maryland by the Bank of England. Thirteen years later William Pinkney, while serving as U.S. Commissioner to England, collected the debt.

As the years passed, Chase, the onetime flaming revolutionist, became more and more conservative. By 1787, he was an active and outspoken Federalist. He was at the vanguard of the opposition to the proposed United States Constitution when it was brought before the Maryland Convention for consideration. However, he had lost much of his popularity and influence by that time and the state convention voted overwhelmingly to ratify the document in 1788.

That same year he was appointed judge of the newly-established criminal court of Baltimore and later received an appointment as chief justice of the general court of Maryland. The General Assembly attempted to remove him from office and, although the motion failed to get the necessary two-thirds vote, a majority of the Assembly felt that his holding two judgeships violated the state constitution.

President Washington submitted Chase's name as an associate justice of the Supreme Court of the United States on January 27, 1796 and on the following day the nomination was confirmed.

During the administration of his old friend John Adams, Chase was a firm advocate of the sedition laws that forbade public expressions of opposition to the law and government of the United States. Adams had used these laws to stifle political opposition from Thomas Jefferson's Democratic-Republican Party.

On May 2, 1803, Justice Chase, appearing before a Baltimore Grand Jury, denounced the adoption of manhood suffrage in Maryland, claiming that it would convert "our Republican Constitution . . . into a mobocracy." He was also reported to have assailed the new Jefferson Administration as "weak, pusillanimous, relaxed."

Through the secret efforts of President Jefferson, impeachment proceedings were brought against Chase and got under way in February, 1805. The key question became whether the term "high crimes and misdemeanors" could be extended to Congress' interpretation of "good behavior." A majority of the Senate found Chase guilty on two of the charges, but because a two-thirds plurality was needed for conviction, he was acquitted.

He remained a member of the Supreme Court until his death at the age of 70 on June 19, 1811.

A large-proportioned six-footer, Chase was described by Chief Justice John Marshall's biographer, A.J. Beveridge, in this manner: "His face was broad and massive, his complexion a brownish red. 'Bacon face' was a nickname applied to him by the Maryland bar. His head was large, his brow wide, and his hair thick and white...."

Supreme Court Justice Joseph Storey, who filled Chase's vacancy on the Court after his death, described his predecessor as a man whose "manners are coarse, and in appearance harsh; but in reality he abounds with good humor.... In person, in manners, in unwieldy strength, in severity of reproof, in real tenderness of heart, and above all in intellect, he is the living, I had almost said the exact, image of Samuel Johnson."

More than two decades after Chase died, Chief Justice John Marshall wrote of his former colleague: "He possessed a strong mind, great legal knowledge, and was a valuable judge, whose loss was seriously felt by his survivors. He was remarkable also for his vivacity and his companionable qualities. He said many things which were much admired at the time, but I have not treasured them in my memory so as to be able to communicate them."

In Annapolis, a reminder of this controversial patriot exists in the Chase-Lloyd House which stands on a plot of land at what is now the corner of Maryland Avenue and King George Street. Sam Chase purchased the property for 100 pounds sterling in 1769 and erected the three-story house on it. The reason the first floor is above the ground is to allow room for an immense wine cellar with a brick barrel vault that runs the full depth of the house.

It is uncertain whether Chase, who sold the entire property in 1771 to Edward Lloyd for 504 pounds sterling, ever occupied the house. But the building came back into the Chase family in 1847 and it has borne the Chase name ever since.

VII

THE VERSATILE GOSSIP DIARIST

Many of our colonial forebears were endowed with astonishing versatility. Benjamin Franklin and Thomas Jefferson, for instance, are best known for their skills in the art of statesmanship, but they were both highly accomplished in myriad other fields of endeavor. A printer by trade, Franklin also excelled as an inventor, scientist, author, publisher and businessman. In addition to writing the Declaration of Independence and serving as the third President of the United States, Jefferson was an extraordinary architect whose achievements include the University of Virginia, the state capitol at Richmond, Va., and Monticello; he also invented the swivel chair and the dumbwaiter, translated the plays of Aeschylus and Sophocles, played the violin well enough to participate in chamber music concerts, and was one of the most successful scientific farmers of his time.

While his accomplishments in no way can be compared to those of Franklin or Jefferson, William Faris may well have been the most versatile citizen of early Annapolis. As Franklin thought of himself as a printer throughout his life, Faris saw himself as a watch- and clockmaker; but the Annapolitan was also one of the most outstanding silversmiths of eighteenth century Maryland as well as a cabinetmaker, designer, dentist, diarist, tavern keeper and tulip grower.

Faris, who was born in London on August 16, 1728, came to Philadelphia as a young man and it was probably there that he learned the watch- and clockmaking trade. He arrived in Annapolis in 1757 to open his watchmaking business and seven years later expanded it to include silversmithing.

He subsequently combined his trades with tavern keeping and operated both businesses on lots presently occupied by 25 and 27 West Street, a tract that extended back to where the dwellings at 98 and 100 Cathedral Street are presently located.

Faris' account books reveal that his customers represented a veritable Who's Who of Annapolis; numbered among them were Charles Carroll, Samuel Chase and William Paca, all signers of the Declaration of Independence, and Anthony Stewart, the prominent but unfortunate merchant whose brig, the *Peggy Stewart,* was burned in the Annapolis version of the Boston Tea Party.

Besides the surviving objects of his several crafts, William Faris is remembered by a series of elegant silverware designs he drafted, a diary in which he logged all the local gossip but also gave an interesting picture of the town from the years 1792-1804, and by a poem called *The Will of William Faris,* which he did not write.

The "will" was obviously intended as a harmless prank by its author, Charlotte Hesselius, daughter of the portrait painter John Hesselius; she was a close friend of Faris' daughters. An unquestionably clever young lady, Charlotte was only nineteen when she wrote the poem in 1790. In 1792, she married Thomas Jennings Johnson, son of Thomas Johnson, Governor of Maryland during the Revolutionary War; she died two years later.

Although it was at first privately circulated, the "will" got out of hand. It caused Faris, whose business was so successful that he had abandoned newspaper advertising for years, to place a notice in the *Maryland Journal and Baltimore General Advertiser* indignantly denying the rumor of his death and the authorship of "a spurious will."

He used the notice to confirm that he was still very much engaged in the business of watch- and clockmaking on West Street in Annapolis.

Miss Hesselius opens the "will" by saying:

> Old Faris one day, as he sat in his shop
> Revolving the chances of dying or not
> The hyppo so seized him he tho't it was best
> To divide his estate ere his soul went to rest,
> So to work went the goldsmith: —Dreadful the task!
> But first, for advice, he applied to his flask.
> The gin, ever generous, fresh spirits afforded
> And the will as I heard it was nearly thus worded. . . .

He leaves to his wife:

> The plates, spoons and dishes, pots, kettles and tables,
> With the red and white cow that inhabits the stables,
> The landscape, and "Judith" that hangs on the wall,
> And the musical clock hind the door in the hall.

His buckles and cane go to his son William, but nothing more because this offspring was a man of some substance and besides:

> The dog grew ungrateful, set up for himself,
> And at Norfolk, they say, he has plenty of pelf.

Faris turns over the tools of his shop to his son Hyram, who also inherits his brown coat with silver buttons (as well as instructions for removing a persistent grease stain from it), his corduroy breeches and a pair of silk hose.

To his son Charles go his watch, his bird organ, a black ring, all the teeth he had pulled since starting the practice of dentistry and six pairs of thread stockings.

His garden utensils and some books are willed to his seafaring son, St. John, along with the wish that he would leave the sea and return to his family.

There is also mention of William Faris' enemies:

> Thank God! I've but two that I hate from my heart,
> And, as ill luck would have it, they're not far apart,
> I've the greatest dislike; God forgive me the sin;
> But indeed there's no bearing that old Allan Quynn,
> There's another I hate bad as Quynn for the fraud
> That his heart is so full of; that's Abraham Claude.

Abraham Claude was Faris' chief business rival and Allan Quynn was Claude's father-in-law. Interestingly enough, the poem was published twice, first in *Scribner's Monthly* in January, 1879, and later in Elihu Riley's *The Ancient City,* and both times fictitious names were inserted for those of Claude and Quynn in order to avoid slandering their families. Thus, Allan Quynn becomes "Louis Dinn" and Abraham Claude is referred to as "Jonathan Todd" in the *Scribner's* and *Ancient City* versions.

In bequeathing the family spinet to Faris' daughter, Nancy, Miss Hesselius goes into some detail about Nancy's frustrations in learning to play that instrument. The teacher was Harry Woodcock, a talented but impoverished man for whom Faris has affection:

> But I still like old Woodcock I vow and declare;
> As a proof I shall leave him a lock of my hair.

Nancy also acquires Faris' Negress slave, Sylva. But Sylva's daughter goes to his daughter Abigail who is to teach her "to spin, knit and sew." And Faris, or Miss Hesselius, even remembers Sol Mogg, the St. Anne's sexton, to whom he wills his "old hat and pipe."

One of the most valuable actual legacies left by William Faris was the diary in which he reported the major and minor news events of the town, his perpetual bickering with his sons, his progress as a tulip grower, the deaths and burials in Annapolis and a good portion of town gossip. To his credit, however, whenever Faris learned that a rumor was untrue he immediately corrected the misinformation. Thus, on the same day we have these two reports:

> Died, his Excellency George Plater, Esq., of Violent Attack of Gaul of the Stomack. A false Report his Excellency is much better and I am hopes he will recover yet.

Faris' accounts sometimes demonstrated a sense of humor:

> Blew very hard. Upset Miss Kittey Fleming on the Stad House Hill, carryed away all her top rigging and brused her face, made her nose bleed.

But his entries can also be downright malicious, such as when he recorded the wedding of an Annapolis couple followed by "and the Town talked that he should have married her sooner as she is with child" and when he tells of Miss Nancy Quynn leaving on the stage for

Baltimore and then to Frederick, adding that "the Town says she is with child and not of her own couler."

We also learn such spicy tidbits as: a quarrel at Mann's Hotel between Captain Kelty and some French officers in which Kelty strikes one of them and swords are drawn but bystanders step in and escort Kelty home; Miss Betsey Wright married a French officer who "has been in town eight or ten days" and that the officer was in her company six or eight times "and cannot speak a word of English nor she one word of French"; an intoxicated Richard Brewer "had a difference" with a young man "who gave him a nock and hurt him a good deal"; Major Wright and General Lloyd fought a duel, Lloyd suffering a wound in the neck and another in the arm while Wright received a slight arm wound; Mrs. Quynn went into the cow pen "and one of the cows poked her and broke her thigh"; and attempts to set "Mr. Peaco's House" and "the Stable of Mrs. Gaters" on fire within three days of one another.

One of Faris' longer accounts concerns a suicide attempt by the wife of John Davidson:

A Negro woman observed her to be very melloncolly, saw her take the key of the Garrett and go up there, one thing she never knew her to do before, after she went up a little wile, the woman followed her very softly, when she came to the Garrett door it was shut, she peep'd through the key hole and saw her mistress hanging clear of the flore. She immediately burst open the Doore and luckely having a knife she cut her down and for the Present saved her Life. Mr. John Davidson was away from home, he and one of his Daughters was gone to dine at Mr. Nich. Worthington's, whose Daughter was married the Day before.

However, a few days later Faris corrected the story by noting: "Mr. Whitcroft told me that it was a false and mallishous storey Rais'd on Mrs. Davidson, it's true that there were some words in the family, she did not want Mr. Davidson and Daughter to go to Worthington's to Dine."

Faris had three daughters; Nancy and Abigail both married sea captains (which is interesting when one considers their father's objections to their brother St. John, who died in 1796 while in command of a ship bound from Baltimore to Amsterdam, choosing a seafaring life), and the third daughter, Rebecca, died unmarried in her early twenties. The diary reflects Faris' apparent devotion to his daughters, but his relationship with his sons is quite another matter. He had four sons and St. John was the only one of them who did not follow the silversmith and watchmaking trades. After a quarrel with his father, the eldest, William, left Maryland and, as previously mentioned, became a successful craftsman and businessman in Norfolk, Va. The other sons, Charles and

Hyram, practiced their trade in Annapolis; but Faris seems to have been constantly at odds with at least one of them.

In his entry of June 4, 1797, Faris reported that his son, Charles, had stopped having breakfast at home but continued to have dinner with the family. However, Faris wrote that Charles "mumbles out something like, how do you do papa in a manner that appears to me that he would rather not speak at all" and that evening Charles left the table without eating his dinner and "never spoke a word to me—nor I to him."

On September 10, we learn of a quarrel between Charles and Hyram in which Faris lets Charles know he was "very much in the Rong and that he had Use Hyram very ill." Faris said he told Charles that he would "never speake to him more" if he did not patch up things with his brother. But Charles took his hat and went off in anger.

However, Faris apparently settled his differences with Charles, who came and helped his father in the yard on March 26, 1799. By the following month, Faris and Hyram were having their problems. On April 2, Hyram moved his chest "from my House to where I don't know." Hyram returned home two days later to bid his mother and sisters farewell, telling them he was going to live in Baltimore; Faris wrote that, "I then told him he might go where he pleased, I had nothing to say to him, he went off." Two months later, Charles, who had been boarding away from home, returned to live in his father's house.

During the last four years the diary was kept, Faris made frequent references to the alcoholic escapades of his apprentice, William McParlin, who was later to become a prominent Annapolis silversmith in his own right. On November 16, 1800, Faris penned this gem:

> Billee Gott Tipsey and in the Evening he told Mrs. Faris that he wanted a candel to transcribe some musick but instead of Transcribing Musick he bundled up his cloathes and went off with him Self. Mr. Pitt and myself went in search of him wee met him in the street by the Ball House, he was very saussey, we brought him home and put him to bed.

The next day Faris asked his apprentice where he had left his clothing and Billee replied that he did not remember. But when Faris took down the "Cow Skin" and threatened him with a "severe whipping," Billee's memory improved and he admitted that he was "at McNemarrows." The apprentice and Faris went there and, after encountering minor resistance, recovered the young man's clothing. Faris wrote that Billee then "promised to behave well for the future and never to do the like again and so I passed it over."

Notwithstanding his solemn pledge to reform, the incorrigible Billee continued to lapse into misbehavior from time to time. On January 12,

1801, Faris discovered that Billee was working on a watch that a customer had given him to repair "on his own account"—a clear violation of the relationship between apprentice and master.

In May of 1802, Faris wrote: "I sent Billee with some letters to the Packett, he got tipsey, I did not discover it he took a Watch to alter her going, I then discovered it but too late he broke the cett off the Verge." On July 30, Faris reported that in the evening "Billee went to see Woodberry at the Play house and came Home very drunk." Apparently the apprentice suffered a rather nasty hangover, for on the following day Faris wrote: "Billee's Unable to do anything to Day."

Faris faithfully kept the diary until August 9, 1804—only a few days before his death. Possibly because of the poem written some 14 years before by Miss Hesselius, he left no will.

VIII

BARNUM'S BIG LESSON

Even the World's Most Fabulous Showman—Phineas T. Barnum—had to learn his trade. And, according to Barnum himself, it was in Annapolis that he was taught one of his most valuable lessons in showmanship.

It all happened back in 1836 when Barnum was a young man traveling the east coast with Aaron Turner, an Englishman who had given America its first full-top canvas circus.

The show featured Signor Vivalla, an Italian immigrant who balanced bayoneted rifles on his nose and who was under personal contract to Barnum.

Barnum, although still in his early twenties, served as ticket seller, treasurer and partner to Turner when the circus made a tour of eastern states.

When the circus reached Annapolis, Turner and Barnum stayed at a local hotel. And on a Sunday morning, Turner was regaling some of the hotel patrons in the restaurant-bar with his colorful repertoire of anecdotes when Barnum, dressed in his Sabbath best, passed through on his way outdoors to have a look at the town.

As Barnum reached the street in front of the hotel, Turner told the others, "I think it's very singular that you permit that rascal to march your streets in open day. It wouldn't be allowed in Rhode Island, and I suppose that is the reason the black-coated scoundrel has come down this way."

Someone in the curious audience asked Turner who the man was. "Don't you know?" boomed Turner. "That is the Reverend E.K. Avery, the murderer of Miss Cornell!"

Sarah Cornell, a 30-year-old factory worker, had been found hanging, apparently murdered, three years earlier outside Tiverton, Rhode Island. Among her effects there was a note that cast suspicion upon the Reverend Ephraim K. Avery, a Methodist minister. Avery became the first clergyman to be tried for murder in the United States. Although he was eventually acquitted, the public disagreed with the verdict and the disgraced minister was forced to leave Rhode Island.

When Aaron Turner claimed that Barnum was Avery, a small group of Annapolitans went after him. By the time they caught up with Barnum, there were more than 100 irate citizens ready to tar and feather the unsuspecting showman; there was also talk of lynching the "culprit." The crowd ripped off Barnum's new coat and shoved him into the dirt while he pleaded for mercy.

Barnum's Big Lesson

"I am not Avery," Barnum pleaded. "I despise that villain. . . . My name is Barnum . . . Old Turner, my partner, has hoaxed you with this ridiculous story."

The angry mob was skeptical, but Barnum managed to persuade cooler heads to take him back to the hotel in order that Turner might reveal his true identity. When they arrived at the hotel, Turner was standing on the porch, shaking with laughter. But he admitted that there might have been "some mistake" in the matter.

After taking a closer look at Barnum, Turner finally said: "The fact is my friend Barnum has a new suit of black clothes on, and it makes him look so much like a priest, I concluded that it must be Avery."

The crowd appreciated the joke at Barnum's expense and quickly dispersed. But Barnum was left with his new coat torn and the rest of his clothing damaged and soiled.

Later Barnum demanded to know why Turner had played such a dangerous trick on him. His partner replied, "My dear Barnum, it was all for our good. Remember, all we need to insure success is notoriety. You will see that this will be noised all about town . . . and our pavilion will be crammed tomorrow night."

Indeed, the Turner-Barnum circus played to a full house the following night.

Barnum went on to unparalleled fame as a circus impresario. He introduced the world to the amazing General Tom Thumb, a 25-inch midget who weighed but 15 pounds; Jumbo, a six-and-a-half-ton elephant whose daily diet consisted of 200 pounds of hay, 15 loaves of bread, and assorted oats, onions, biscuits and fruits, washed down by five pails of water and a quart of whiskey (his fans included Queen Victoria, Theodore Roosevelt and Winston Churchill); as well as the two Wild Men of Borneo (who were actually Hiram and Barney Davis of Long Island), and America's First Marimba Band, which Henry M. Stanley supposedly brought out of Africa after finding Livingstone at Ujiji, but which Barnum had, in reality, recruited from New York's Bowery.

Barnum's most notable quote during a long and colorful career was, "There's a sucker born every minute." He was aware that the public loves a shrewd and clever hoax. And, in Annapolis at the age of 25, Phineas T. Barnum learned his big lesson when the hoax was played on him.

IX

OLD JOE MORGUE

One of the more interesting town characters of nineteenth-century Annapolis was Joseph Simmons, who was sometimes called "Joe Morgue." He was the sexton of St. Anne's Church and at his death in August, 1836, Simmons was said to be at least 100 years old.

According to the newspaper obituary, he was the oldest inhabitant of Annapolis at the time. The newspaper account proclaimed:

"Not one man that ever has been a member of the Legislature, Executive, or Superior Judiciary of the State of Maryland, not a student of St. John's College, or a scholar of our humbler schools, but will remember the well known summons which his bell gave them alternately to duties and to relaxation. Alas! old Joe rings no more."

Renowned for his punctuality, Simmons was said to have rung the town bell late on only one occasion, and that one instance turned out to be a testimonial to his chivalry. A lady who told him her husband insisted on having his lunch at one o'clock sharp pleaded with him to wait until she arrived home before sounding the bell. Advising her to "walk fast," Simmons consented to her wish.

The obituary claims that it was at gravedigging that Simmons "enjoyed the distinction of having held an office longer than perhaps any man ever did, nay, possibly ever will do, in this state."

The account emphasizes that "many peculiarities of character ... distinguished the deceased" and that he was "even thought of with a strange superstition, awe and aversion by some 'grown up children.' ..."

Simmons must have been quite a sight as he tottered down the streets of Annapolis with his white hair flowing over his shoulders. It was said that he lacked only the emblematic scythe to present the apparition of Father Time himself.

Children were convinced they were doomed if Simmons looked at one of them and announced: "I want you." When they confronted Simmons they would put on their best behavior and inquire politely: "How do, Mr. Morgue?" Whereupon Simmons, who despised that nickname, flew into a rage that immediately threw the youngsters into a state of bewilderment and shock.

As the years passed, Joe Morgue's eccentricities seemed to multiply. When the mood struck him, he was inclined to walk down the street and hiss at an innocent passerby: "I'll have you some day." It was as if he convinced himself that he held in his hands the power of life and death.

When a clergyman would conclude his graveside service, Simmons would sign it off with his own hearty: "Amen." On one such occasion, Parson Wyatt was reading the funeral service when some boys offended Simmons, who, in turn, vented his wrath in some rather salty language. The minister and the sexton finished speaking together and Simmons shouted: "Amen!"

After the funeral attendants left the cemetery, the parson shook his cane in Simmons' face, saying: "Don't you ever dare to stand along side of me again and say amen to any service I perform."

Pointing to the opposite end of the grave, Simmons angrily retorted: "Well then, go over on the other side."

Then there was a man named Jeffrey who lived at the foot of Duke of Gloucester Street and was periodically inclined to falling into a comatose state. Several times, Jeffrey was prepared for interment, always awakening in time to prevent the funeral. However, Jeffrey was once actually lowered into the grave when noises were heard from inside his coffin. Informed by frantic mourners that Jeffrey was alive, Joe Morgue continued filling the grave saying: "He's got to die sometime; and if he is not dead, he ought to be."

X

BAD DAY AT CRABTOWN

It is doubtful that anyone who spent the day in Annapolis on July 5, 1847 ever really forgot it. Tempers flared, fistfights broke out, bricks and rocks were hurled back and forth between opposing crowds, shots were fired. The entire town was a tinderbox.

It all began peacefully enough with a steamer pulling into the city dock. More than 700 passengers were aboard. They were on their way to St. Michael's in Talbot County to celebrate the anniversary of America's independence. Among them were two rifle companies—the Eagle Artillerists, led by Colonel George P. Kane and the Columbian Riflemen, commanded by Captain Robert McAllister.

The boat was some four hours out of Baltimore when her skipper, Captain Sutton, found that the creaky craft could not cross the Chesapeake Bay because it was overloaded.

Captain Sutton brought the boat into Annapolis and tried to convince 150 or so of the passengers to disembark and return to Baltimore as best they could. When no one would go ashore, Sutton refused to proceed across the Bay.

Gradually passengers began leaving the boat. Some visited the Naval Academy and others went to the State House; they were received cordially in both places.

However, according to one eyewitness account, "With some of the community there appeared to be something wrong, as if some past offense had not been forgotten or some new aggression had been committed."

A Baltimore youth broke a window on Church Street. While William F. Smith, of Baltimore, was paying for it, one of the crowd was arrested by an Annapolis constable. Although this aroused the anger of the Baltimore boys, Smith convinced them to return to the boat.

But several members of the visiting party entered the old City Hotel (now the Masonic temple at 162 Conduit Street), went to the kitchen and helped themselves to dinner. Because of their rowdy manner, Colonel John Walton, the proprietor of the hotel, threatened to send them to jail and they left.

In other parts of town, curses were shouted and pistols were shot. Later Colonel Kane said he left the boat at Annapolis and exchanged his uniform for civilian clothing. He was determined to return to Baltimore by railway because the conduct of some of those aboard the boat was so disorderly.

While dining in Annapolis, Colonel Kane heard firearms being discharged and left at once for the steamer. Before Kane reached the boat,

Bad Day at Crabtown

Judge Nicholas Brewer, of Annapolis, who had learned that the son of a friend was involved in an altercation, was already at the wharf.

Judge Brewer later explained that he "saw by the soiled state of the clothes of the young man and the injury he had received on his nose, that he had been engaged in a fight." After persuading the youth to leave the wharf, the judge sensed enough hostility in the air to suspect the possibility that a full-scale riot might emerge. He decided to stay at the wharf to prevent any more trouble from occurring.

The situation appeared relatively calm for the next hour as the boat prepared to leave Annapolis. But then the crowd on the steamer became restless; somebody shouted to bring "that big-bellied man with the straw hat" on board. A prominent Annapolitan, Daniel T. Hyde, overheard the shouting from the porch of his home some 100 yards from the dock. Hyde went to the wharf assuming that Judge Brewer might need help. However, the judge seemed to be in no immediate danger.

Soon Annapolis citizens on the wharf and Baltimore passengers on the steamer were exchanging profanities. A few of the Baltimore boys ran ashore, picked up stones and retreated to the boat. Two men advanced from the gangway leading to the wharf and appeared ready to fight. But Judge Brewer persuaded them to return to the boat. Hyde assisted with the lines and the steamer cast off.

Suddenly two halves of a lemon were thrown into the crowd from the boat. An unidentified dark object was also hurled from the steamer. The Annapolitans responded with a barrage of bricks. Baltimoreans began throwing stones and firing pistols.

As bricks hurled from the shore fell among the women and children aboard the boat, soldiers on the steamer ran for the room where their rifles were stored. Captain McAllister sent one of his men to guard the rifles, but by that time passengers were already removing rifles and pushing aside anyone who tried to stop them. Some ladies aboard the boat panicked and jumped overboard.

Meanwhile on the wharf, Judge Brewer and Mr. Hyde were trapped in the crossfire. Kicking aside two boys who were throwing stones, Hyde tried to warn the Baltimoreans that the boat was in danger of running aground on an old stone wall in the water near the wharf.

Running to the end of the dock, he called to Captain McAllister to throw the stern line ashore so he could help the boat negotiate a turn and avoid hitting the wall. Misunderstanding Hyde's intentions, Captain McAllister drew his sword and threatened the Annapolitan, who kept trying to make the captain understand his friendly offer.

At the same time, Judge Brewer grabbed a young man attempting to fire a pistol at the boat. Glasses, bottles and stones began flying in the air towards the crowd on the wharf. John W. Brady, who had taken the gun-wielding youth from the judge, was shot.

Constable John Lamb came to the judge's assistance in attempting to quell the riot. Someone on the steamer shouted, "Shoot that officer, I mistrust him." Three rifles were leveled at the judge who ducked behind a woodpile to protect himself. One of the rifles was fired.

In all, it was estimated that there were 20 rifle shots from the boat and two pistol shots and two gunshots from the shore. Five Annapolitans were injured: T.C. Loockerman was slightly wounded by a shot in the leg; Basil McNew was badly wounded by a shot in the side; John W. Brady was shot through both legs and seriously injured; Edward Barroll was seriously wounded in the side; and Watkins Hall lost two toes.

According to Hyde's testimony at the investigation of the incident, when Hall and Loockerman, who had been throwing stones, fell, "the people on board the boat hurrahed enough for an election day."

Word of the riot spread rapidly through Annapolis. Powder was contributed by a local merchant and a cannon was seized by citizens who hurried to the wharf to avenge the assault on their townsmen.

To make matters worse, the steamer was now wedged between the two sides of the narrow wharf. Trying to escape the volleys from the shore, passengers ran to the opposite side of the boat, nearly capsizing the craft.

The crowd on the wharf brought the cannon into position. Colonel Kane, who remained ashore, attempted to talk the Annapolitans out of firing it. When they would not listen, he courageously threw one arm over the breach, placed his other hand over the muzzle and declared that if the cannon were discharged, he would be blown to bits.

The colonel was warned that the cannon was double-shotted and loaded. Some Annapolitans struggled with Kane to force him away from the weapon. During the struggle, someone whispered in the colonel's ear that the cannon had been spiked. It was the voice of Judge Brewer, who had taken the resourceful precaution of spiking the weapon with his toothpick. Brewer halted two more attempts to load the cannon.

Hyde described the loading of the cannon as "a mere farce . . . a scene of complete confusion, some wanting to do one thing and others another and, in the meanwhile, the boat was fast getting out of their reach even if it had been loaded."

Heaping praise upon Brewer, Hyde said the judge "did all that any man could do" to suppress the crowd, adding that if the duties performed that day pertained to his office as judge that he (Hyde) would have no part of it for "twice its salary." Hyde further maintained that Brewer, in his endeavors to keep the peace, was "in imminent danger of his life."

Despite a full judicial investigation, none of the participants was indicted. But Annapolitans who were there long remembered that day of excitement, turmoil and fear.

XI

THE GOVERNOR'S LADY

One of the most remarkable and able governors of Maryland during the nineteenth century was Francis Thomas, whose brilliant political career came into collision with a sensational marital scandal that very probably prevented his being elected President of the United States.

The jealous and unpredictable chief executive who occupied the State House in Annapolis from 1842 to 1845 went as far as to print his own version of his domestic difficulties in a 52-page pamphlet which he had distributed to members of the General Assembly and Maryland representatives in Congress.

A native of Frederick County, Thomas came to Annapolis for his education. He graduated from St. John's College and returned to Frederick in 1819 to practice law and begin his meteoric rise in politics. Three years later, at the age of 23, he was elected to the Maryland House of Delegates; by the time he was 30, he was elected Speaker of the House.

In March, 1831, Thomas was elected to the United States Congress and served there for ten years, rising to the chairmanship of the powerful judiciary committee before he was elected governor in 1841.

He established a reputation for oratorical brilliance and a fiery temper. The latter prompted him to challenge a political enemy to a duel at 12 paces. Thomas apparently aimed his verbal barbs more sharply than he did his pistol and, fortunately, his opponent's marksmanship was equally as poor; each fired one shot and they both missed.

While he was a member of Congress, Thomas resided in a Washington boarding house with the family of Missouri Senator Thomas H. Benton, brother-in-law of Virginia Governor James McDowell. In 1836, Governor McDowell sent his eldest daughter, Sally Campbell Preston McDowell, then 15 years old, to live with her aunt and uncle while attending school in Georgetown.

Five years later and seven months prior to his inauguration as Governor of Maryland, Thomas, after persistent encouragement from the Bentons, was married to Miss McDowell at her father's home in Virginia. Thomas was 42 and his bride was 20.

Shortly after the wedding, his troubles began. He became embroiled in a quarrel with Governor McDowell and Senator Benton, who made serious charges regarding his character and even questioned his sanity. They accused him of locking his wife in her chambers when he was absent from his home, which he flatly denied. They also charged that while on his honeymoon in Virginia, Thomas had gone to bed with a pair of pistols and told his new wife he would use one on her father and the other on her brother.

Thomas admitted possession of the weapons, staunchly insisting, however, that he kept them in a trunk in his carriage and that he never brought them into the house—much less to bed. He further admitted having commented in a jocular vein to another gentleman—but not to his wife—that he would use one of the pistols on his father-in-law and one on his brother-in-law.

Once Governor Thomas was addressing the Maryland Legislature and, seeing Governor McDowell and Senator Benton in the audience, mentioned his marital problems.

He said before the entire General Assembly that the McDowell women "were of the best type of American motherhood" and that his own wife was "as pure as the icicle from the frozen north." But he then aimed his merciless tongue at the McDowell men: "They have followed me through the trackless forest like the hell-hounds of perdition.... Let them come! I fear them not—from Bully Benton to Blackguard McDowell."

At the conclusion of the proceedings, Governor Thomas personally escorted his wife to the train and she returned to her father's household in Virginia.

Thomas' rebuttal to the charges leveled against him by Governor McDowell was contained in a pamphlet entitled, "Statement of Francis Thomas," in which he made repeated accusations about his wife's adulterous behavior with her cousin, a nephew of Governor McDowell.

Several days after the wedding, the cousin showed up in Frederick. Thomas wrote that he "perceived an intimacy between him (the cousin) and Mrs. Thomas which I did not like, on account of my knowledge of his want of delicacy towards another lady...." Here, Governor Thomas was referring to an incident in Virginia in which he claimed that he saw the cousin "attempt what I deemed gross liberties with a young lady, who was entitled to his particular respect...."

Governor Thomas maintained that his bride and her cousin held "contrived interviews ... out of my presence." He said he chose to ignore the situation at first because he "looked upon her participation in those proceedings as, perhaps, an attempt to make me jealous."

But when these "interviews" continued and Governor Thomas confronted his wife with his displeasure, she sent her cousin a strongly worded note demanding that he leave Maryland.

Governor Thomas said that on the very night he arrived in Annapolis to assume his duties as Governor in January, 1842, a young man was with Mrs. Thomas "in the private chambers of (Government House) ... for a long time, while I was sitting with other company in the parlour."

The spectacular marital quarrel was believed to be the reason Governor Thomas was not nominated for the Presidency at the Democratic National Convention held in Baltimore in 1844. Thomas was said to be a leading contender for the nomination, but Governor McDowell headed the Virginia delegation and was active in opposition to his son-in-law's candidacy. Thomas was never even considered formally by the convention which instead chose James K. Polk, who was eventually elected President of the United States.

Approximately a year after his gubernatorial term expired, Thomas was granted a divorce from his wife. His behavior became extremely erratic, alternating between attempts at reconciliation and condemnations of her in very harsh words. She later married the Reverend John Miller, one of the most distinguished Presbyterian clergymen of his time.

Some 16 years after he left the State House, Thomas made a political comeback. He again served in Congress from 1861-1869, but it was a far cry from the ambition that once seemed well within his grasp.

He later served two years as Collector of Internal Revenue for the District of Maryland and resigned in 1872 to accept the post of United States Minister to Peru. Returning to Western Maryland in 1875 to a mountainside farm in Garrett County, Thomas attempted to breed Alpaca sheep imported from South America.

While surveying his property on January 22, 1876, he was struck by a locomotive, thrown 20 feet and killed instantly, thus ending the long career of one of Maryland's most colorful and eccentric politicians.

XII

THE GENERAL WHO SEIZED ANNAPOLIS

On April 19, 1861, the Sixth Massachusetts Militia was traveling south on its way to fight in the Civil War when it encountered an angry secessionist mob numbering from 8,000 to 10,000 in Baltimore. Stones and brickbats were hurled at the last two cars of the troop train. Several of the soldiers suffered minor injuries, eight were seriously wounded and three were killed. Many of the militiamen fired back, killing several Baltimoreans.

The news of the Baltimore riot reached General Benjamin Butler who was in Philadelphia with his Eighth Massachusetts Militia. Communications between Washington and Philadelphia had been cut off and Butler, fearing that the Confederates had crossed the Potomac, was determined to take his troops to the nation's capital.

Deciding to bypass Baltimore, Butler transported his 700 men by rail to Perryville, Maryland, on the northern bank of the Susquehanna River. He then commandeered the *Maryland,* a steam-powered ferryboat that had been used to transfer passengers across the river, and proceeded to Annapolis. Butler left Philadelphia on April 20, and anchored around midnight two miles off Annapolis where he observed the Naval Academy illuminated.

Officials at the Academy had heard rumors that southern sympathizers planned to take a boat from Baltimore and seize the Naval Academy. These fears were compounded by rockets flaring across the skies from the direction of Baltimore, and the sudden appearance of the steamer. At the same time, Butler believed that the Academy had been captured by the Confederates.

Meanwhile Captain Blake, the superintendent of the Academy, had been ordered by Secretary of Navy Gideon Welles to defend the schoolship *Constitution* "at all hazards" and to destroy the vessel if she could not be defended.

With the appearance of the *Maryland,* general quarters were sounded on the *Constitution,* and the four 32-pounders on board the Academy ship were run out at her stern.

From the *Constitution* came the call: "Ship ahoy! What ship is that?"

"Ship ahoy!" replied the *Maryland.* "Keep off, or I will sink you."

Fortunately the tension was broken when a voice came from Butler's boat that was recognized on the Academy ship, saying: "For God's sake, don't fire; we are friends." It was the Academy chaplain who had been on leave and was returning with the militiamen.

Within a short time, Lieutenant Mathews, an aide to the Academy superintendent boarded the *Maryland* with a message from Maryland Governor Thomas Hicks advising against landing troops in Annapolis. "The excitement is very great, and I think it prudent that you should take your men elsewhere," wrote Hicks. "I have declared to the Secretary of War advising against your landing your men here."

Butler sent his aide, Captain Peter Haggerty, to accompany Lt. Mathews to see the Governor and dispatched his brother, Andrew Jackson Butler, a member of his staff, ashore in civilian clothes to make a reconnaissance of the town.

The next morning, Superintendent Blake boarded Butler's vessel and pleaded with the General: "Thank God! Thank God! Won't you save the *Constitution?*"

Unaware that Blake was referring to the ship, not the document, Butler's answer was, "Yes, that is just what I am here for!"

Subsequently Butler learned of Captain Blake's concern about the ship which was aground at her moorings and did not have an ample crew to sail out of the harbor. Apprised of the situation, the General said he had "plenty of sailor men from the town of Marblehead, where their fathers built the *Constitution*." He was evidently ignorant of the fact that the *Constitution* was actually built in Boston.

Despite Governor Hicks' protests, Bradley's only recourse was to land his troops in Annapolis; the undisciplined militiamen under his command had already consumed their three days' rations before reaching Perryville, and there was not enough of the foul-tasting water that had been stored in whiskey kegs aboard the boat to last through the day.

The General sent word to Hicks that he needed supplies along with a request to land his men and allow them passage through the state "on my way to Washington, respecting private property, and paying for what I receive, and outraging the rights of none. . . ." Bradley added, in a postscript, that he believed it "entirely proper" to disembark his troops at the Naval Academy. However, the note requesting permission to land was not delivered until both the Eighth Massachusetts and the Seventh New York Militia, under Colonel Marshall Lefferts, had already been put ashore at the Academy wharf.

Midshipmen from the *Constitution* were landed under arms; they were stationed at the Academy gate all day long to protect the disembarkation and prevent any assault on the Academy by secessionists.

A line in the rear of the midshipmen's quarters was formed by the soldiers who stacked arms and posted sentries. Although neither side fired a shot, there was a considerable amount of tension; southern partisans tossed stones over the Academy wall and the soldiers pitched them back. Meanwhile, the magazines of the *Constitution* had been mined and she would have been blown up before surrendering to the rebels.

General Butler was invited to breakfast at the superintendent's quarters and it was there that he came face to face with Governor Hicks and Annapolis Mayor John R. Magruder. Governor Hicks told Bradley the State of Maryland would not interfere with the landing of the remainder of the troops, but that they must encamp three or four miles outside the city. Mayor Magruder told him the city council had voted against taking action against the Federal troops and urged Butler to march his men out of town immediately.

The General asked if they would furnish him with supplies. They refused and said that he could not purchase anything in Annapolis. He then asked if he could be furnished with transportation to Washington; they told him there were not five horses remaining in town and that the railroad company had taken up their tracks, which was permissible since it was private property.

Telling them that his men could not possibly march without supplies, the General added a note of warning: that while Annapolis authorities apparently were unwilling or unable to control a mob from forming in the town, his own troops were "also very much excited because of the murder of their brothers at Baltimore."

He made it abundantly clear that he planned to remain in Annapolis as long as he found it necessary and that he would march only when he was good and ready.

"If we are attacked we will repel the attack," Butler cautioned, "and there are none that we shall be more happy to see than a representation of the murderers of Baltimore whenever and wherever they visit us. While we stay in Annapolis, if the citizens choose not to have any collision with us, there must be on their part neither stray bricks nor fugitive shots, thrown at us."

A short while later Butler discovered that some railroad tracks outside of town had been torn up and rendered impassable. He sent some of his men to repair the tracks along with troops to stand guard during the reconstruction.

Meanwhile, the General also found a rusty, partly dismantled locomotive locked in a building and he asked if any of his men knew anything about trains. One of the men, Charles Homans, stepped forward and said that not only did he know something about locomotives but this particular engine had been built in the shop where he worked as a civilian; he said he was able to repair it.

While the repairs were under way, Butler requisitioned locomotives and cars from Philadelphia. And since freight boats were bringing more troops into Annapolis, he had an auxiliary track built from the Naval Academy dock across town to the main railroad track.

Once the road was opened, the General sent the Seventh New York and the Eighth Massachusetts militias on to Washington; he remained behind to command the movement of additional troops arriving in Annapolis by boat.

On April 23, Governor Hicks wrote Butler that he had been informed that the General had taken military possession of the Annapolis and Elk-Ridge Railroad. The Governor said: "I deem it my duty to protest against this step—because without at present assigning any other reason, I am informed that such occupation of said railroad will prevent the members of the Legislature from reaching this city."

General Butler answered that it was true his men had taken the railroad, adding: "It might have escaped your notice, but at the official meeting which was had between Your Excellency and the Mayor of Annapolis and the Committee of the Government and myself, as to my landing of troops, it was expressly stated as the reason why I should not land that my troops could not pass the railroad because the company had taken up the rails, and they were private property. It is difficult to see how it could be that if my troops could not pass over the railroad one way the members of the Legislature could pass the other way."

Butler also told the Governor of his intention "to save and not to destroy" and that he did not want to be "under the painful necessity of encumbering your beautiful city while the Legislature is in session."

Governor Hicks was not the bungling dolt or the thinly disguised southern partisan he seemed. He personally supported the Union, but he had a staggering problem: the Maryland General Assembly had not yet voted upon the question of seceding or remaining within the Union. The Governor knew that the border state of Maryland was divided on the issue which was to be settled at the approaching session of the Legislature.

It would have been a delicate position for any governor, but even more so for the governor of a state in such close proximity to the nation's capital and one whose sister state, Virginia, had already joined the Confederacy. Thus, Hicks behavior can be explained quite simply: he did not want to offend or antagonize the legislators with the presence of Federal troops in the state capital at a time when this momentous decision was to be made.

General Butler was preparing himself to join his troops in Washington when he received formal orders from Lieutenant General Winfield Scott on April 25 to command the "Department of Annapolis." His major duty was to keep rail communications open between the nation's capital and Annapolis.

President Lincoln had issued orders to defend Annapolis in the event the Maryland Legislature should choose the course of secession and arm the state against the Federal Government. Lincoln ordered Butler to take prompt and efficient countermeasures in this eventuality "even if necessary to the bombardment of their cities, and, in the extremest necessity, suspension of the writ of habeas corpus."

Governor Hicks chose to convene the General Assembly in Frederick in order to avoid having the legislators feel their decision was being made under duress—in occupied territory, as it were. Butler warned the Governor that he would not tolerate a move towards secession; Hicks reassured him that Maryland would not secede and even entrusted the Great Seal of Maryland to his care so that even if a secession ordinance were enacted, the Seal could not be affixed and it would be illegal.

Governor Hicks also conveyed to Butler his fear that the appearance of Union forces in Maryland would lead to a revolt of slaves in the state. In a letter to the Governor, Butler said he would gladly cooperate in the thwarting of any such uprising. Governor Andrew of Massachusetts reprimanded Butler for this statement. But the General explained his position:

"I had promised to put down a white mob and to preserve and enforce the laws against that. Ought I to allow a black one any preference in the breach of the laws? . . . The question seemed to me to be neither military nor political and was not to be so treated. It was simply a question of good faith and honesty of purpose. The benign effect of my course was instantly seen. The good but timid people of Annapolis, who had fled from their houses at our approach, immediately returned; business resumed its accustomed channels; quiet and order prevailed in the city; confidence took the place of distrust, friendship of enmity, brotherly kindness of sectional hate, and I believe today there is no city in the Union more loyal than the city of Annapolis."

Butler felt so secure in Annapolis that he sent for his wife, Sarah, who was at home in Massachusetts, and his daughter, Blanche, who was attending a convent school in Georgetown, to join him.

The General remained in command at Annapolis until the middle of May. The city was used later during the Civil War as a mobilization point for Union expeditions against Port Royal and Roanoke Island; it was also utilized as a hospital center for wounded Federal troops who occupied buildings at the Naval Academy and on the St. John's College campus, and as a reception facility for exchanged war prisoners. But throughout the war Annapolis never again experienced anything remotely resembling the excitement that was brought when a flamboyant General landed and seized the city from under the nose of a frightened and frantic Governor.

C'est la Guerre, You Rebs!

XIII

C'EST LA GUERRE, YOU REBS!

At the outbreak of the Civil War, the sentiments of Annapolis citizens were clearly on the side of the south; most of the townsfolk were confident the Old Line State would secede from the Union.

The city cast 525 votes for four candidates in the presidential election of 1860, but only one of these was for the victorious Abraham Lincoln, who was bound and determined to preserve the Union. When Maryland decided to remain in the Union, many young Annapolis men chose to run off and join the Confederate Army. Annapolis Mayor John R. Magruder issued strong pleas against landing Federal troops on the banks of the Severn River because he felt certain such action would touch off a riot in the city. In a turnabout version of the Barbara Fritchie story, a woman residing on State Circle hung a Confederate flag from her window as Federal troops paraded below.

But none of these factors lessened the excitement and admiration Annapolitans felt when the dashing, devil-may-care "D'Epeneuil's Zouaves" arrived in town on November 18, 1861.

The Zouaves, more formally known as the 53rd New York Infantry, were a group of Union soldiers—mostly foreigners—so eager to do battle against the Confederacy that they occasionally clobbered each other.

They were a spectacularly colorful lot in their baggy blue trousers, yellow leggings, bright blue blouses with yellow facing and red fezzes with long yellow tassels.

Actually these dazzling uniforms were somewhat conservative for their personal taste; the Zouaves' initial choice of red trousers instead of blue was vetoed by the Secretary of War who wisely figured the more striking color would make them splendid targets for Johnny Reb's itchy trigger fingers.

Still the Zouaves brightened the landscape at their camp on the outskirts of Annapolis in what is now the Parole area.

Some had served in the famous French Foreign Legion and came from Europe to New York, where the entire regiment was recruited; they were lured by the smell of adventure and the need for a change of scenery. Others probably left the Old World because the gendarmes had been breathing uncomfortably down their necks and the Union Army seemed a convenient place to lose one's identity. Still others were recruited from the foreign quarters of New York City. The regiment was predominantly French with a sprinkling of Italians, Belgians, Germans, Spaniards and English.

The Zouaves were commanded by Colonel Lionel J. D'Epeneuil; next in rank was Lieutenant Colonel Joseph A. Viguer de Monteil.

Junior officers included: DeFleau, another Frenchman; Vistang, a Belgian; Cypreini, an Italian, and three Englishmen, Fox, Holden and Coffin.

This melting pot regiment began to form in New York on August 27, 1861 and by November 15, the men had completed their fundamental military training. Three days later they arrived in Annapolis and to the glee of the city's youngsters and the delight of the young ladies in town, they marched through the streets to their campsite approximately two miles from the city.

On a farm owned by James Welch, they erected barracks, dug wells and squatted. One of the wells they dug behind the Welch farmhouse was 65 feet deep, carefully bricked and yielded an abundant supply of water compared to the purest and sweetest found in the entire state.

Not long after their arrival, the Zouaves established a personal reputation as colorful as their uniforms. They were lusty, brawling, drinking men who played and worked hard. They held nightly poker sessions and on Christmas Day, 1861, nearly all of them got outrageously drunk; a scuffle followed in which one of the men was killed.

But quarreling was not restricted to the enlisted ranks. Colonel D'Epeneuil and Viguer de Monteil also had their differences. So much so that they agreed to fight a duel. Junior officers stepped in and prevented it, but the two commanding officers remained cool to one another. It was probably fortunate for D'Epeneuil that the duel was canceled because his own credentials as a fighting man were suspect; however, there was no doubt that Viguer de Monteil, a battle-hardened veteran who was expert with both pistol and sword, could hold his own.

While this happy-go-lucky contingent was camping near Annapolis, some of their officers grew curious about certain members of the enlisted personnel who were slender, young persons never known to shave although they were beardless. Called to headquarters for questioning, they coyly confessed they were not young men at all but young French women who had dressed in the regiment's uniforms so they could be near their lovers. Taking a dim view of this situation, D'Epeneuil promptly shipped the women back to New York.

On January 3, 1862, the regiment received orders to join General Burnside's command at Fortress Monroe, located at the tip of the Virginia peninsula. They were to be assigned to General Parke's Third Brigade.

Annapolis was once again treated to the sparkling spectacle of the Zouaves as they flamboyantly marched en masse to the city wharf two days later. The entire regiment, comprised of 700 men, boarded the sailing ship *John Trucks,* which promptly ran aground on shoals off Horn Point.

After the ship was towed off the shoals, the captain set her course directly for Hatteras Inlet. The revised plan was to join General Burnside's 12,000-man army and capture Roanoke Island where Confederate batteries and a mosquito fleet defended the back door to the strategically significant cities of Norfolk and Richmond.

As luck would have it, the *John Trucks* reached Hatteras Inlet during a storm that made it impossible for the rough and eager Zouaves to land. Only a small detachment which included D'Epeneuil and Viguer de Monteil made it ashore. General Burnside ordered the bulk of the regiment back to Fortress Monroe, but Viguer de Monteil and a few of the men remained with Burnside's forces.

Colonel D'Epeneuil had other ideas. Instead of returning to Fortress Monroe, he brought his troops all the way back to Annapolis. There the colonel wrote a scorching letter to his superiors expressing his disapproval of the way the war was being run. The letter prompted the War Department to break up the regiment.

On February 8, 1862, at the battle of Roanoke Island, Viguer de Monteil, who had become an officer without a command, persuaded General Parke to allow him to fight as a common soldier. This he did in exemplary fashion. At the front, he fired his rifle at the enemy with the steady aim of the true professional he was, pausing only to shout words of encouragement to his comrades in arms. Near the end of the battle, he was shot through the head by a Confederate bullet.

General Parke posthumously commended the Frenchman for displaying "the most marked courage under fire."

It has been said of Viguer de Monteil, the consummate soldier of fortune who had no known political convictions, that had he landed in Charleston instead of New York on his arrival in America, he most probably would have given his life for the Confederacy instead of the Union.

It is interesting to note that when "D'Epeneuil's Zouaves" were disbanded as a regiment in Annapolis, Company A was transferred as a group to the 17th New York Infantry and the remainder of the men were divided between the 132nd and 162nd New York Infantry. Since all three of these fighting units established good battlefield records, it is reasonable to assume that the Zouaves had not been a ragtag array of comic-opera misfits in fancy uniforms but merely mismanaged under the chronic complaining antics of Colonel D'Epeneuil.

XIV

DAYS OF DESPERATION

The maintenance of prisoners was a gigantic headache to both the Union and the Confederacy during the early part of the Civil War. Since neither side had adequate facilities to hold thousands of captives for any length of time, it had become common practice almost from the outset of the war to exchange prisoners shortly after they were captured.

However, once these men were returned other serious problems arose. They were generally sent back to their homes until they could be reassigned; but the system proved unworkable. Disillusioned and frightened by their first taste of combat, many ex-prisoners were furloughed and never heard from again. Homesick soldiers eagerly permitted themselves to be captured in the hope of being paroled and sent home.

To resolve this situation, the Union's War Department issued a general order canceling all furloughs for erstwhile prisoners. Under this order, all men from New England and the Middle Atlantic states' regiments were to be sent to Annapolis; men from the other states were destined for either Jefferson Barracks in Missouri or Camp Chase in Ohio.

In the summer of 1862, some 2,000 soldiers who had been released by the South, arrived in Annapolis. Because they were virtually being held as prisoners by their own government and deprived of the opportunity to return home, their moods ranged from discontent to downright hostility.

Initially, they were to be quartered behind the buildings on the St. John's College campus. But due to insufficient space and the proximity to the temptations of the city, it was necessary to relocate the men at a site two miles southwest of Annapolis on the South River.

The soldiers generally arrived in the same clothing and shoes they wore when they were captured. Furthermore, under the first commandant of Camp Parole, there was not a sufficient supply of blankets and tents to go around.

In late August, supplies arrived and were distributed as rapidly as possible, and a hospital was established. Lieutenant Colonel George E. Sangster, of the 47th New York State Militia, was brought in to take charge of the camp.

He was immediately faced with the seemingly insurmountable task of feeding and clothing the constant flow of new arrivals and those already in camp were depressed and homesick. The soldiers were becoming rowdy; they frequently strayed from camp and wandered into Annapolis where their behavior annoyed and sometimes terrified the local gentry.

Compounding these difficulties was the fact that there were only 90 guards for the first 2,000 men. When the camp population burgeoned to 7,000, there were only 300 guards. Furthermore, the officers among the ex-prisoners considered themselves absolved from military duty and did not feel obliged to help Sangster maintain order and discipline at the camp.

The South River location proved to be very impractical. Wood, clothing, food and medical supplies had to be hauled from Annapolis by mule teams over dirt roads. While the roads could be negotiated with relative ease during the summer, it was rough going in the winter months when snow and mud made the route almost impassable.

As dreary as this might seem, the diary of one Lieutenant Richardson, of the 126th New York Volunteers, who had a brief stay at the camp, records that it was not a total disaster for all the men detained there. Richardson wrote that most of his men had never before seen salt water and that they thoroughly enjoyed the swimming, fishing, crabbing and oystering.

Sangster, an apparently topflight administrator, began shaping up the camp. He instituted military routine with reveille at 5 a.m., breakfast at 6 a.m. and taps at 9 p.m. While his order to cancel all passes to Annapolis must have deepened the anguish of already dissatisfied soldiers, it was unquestionably necessary to prevent desertions and unpleasant episodes from occurring in the town.

While Lieutenant Colonel Sangster was doing his utmost to make the best of a horrendous situation, he was appalled at the large number of ill and injured soldiers who were sent to his camp. Some were even being carried from steamboats and trains on stretchers. Because of the limited hospital facilities, the sick and wounded were sharing tents with healthy men. In November, Sangster complained to Washington about this "inhuman practice."

The issuance of passes to Annapolis was resumed in December, but the men were absolutely prohibited from leaving camp without them. A strict order was handed down that forbade gambling and the use of liquor within the confines of the camp.

There were rumors of heavy gambling and that whiskey was being sold in the camp. There were tales that men were being robbed and even murdered in their sleep. Desertions made it nearly impossible for Sangster to determine whether a man was dead or absent without leave. The rumors continued and the word passed that at least six men had been slain and buried in the night.

An investigation was held on December 7 and 8 to determine the validity of the allegations of murder, gambling and the sale of liquor. Thirteen witnesses testified that liquor was sold and that certain tents had been converted into makeshift gambling dens, but all denied knowledge of any murders.

By the winter of 1862-63, the men were living in tents heated by stoves that were fueled by wood brought from Annapolis. However, since the wagons bringing in the wood were frequently hijacked by the soldiers, some tents had plentiful supplies of wood while others had hardly enough to make it through the cold weather.

In addition, tents were wearing out through exposure to the weather; when a tent was temporarily vacated, it was frequently stolen to double the roof of another tent.

By February 1, 1863, the efficient and resourceful Lieutenant Colonel Sangster had wooden barracks with floors and stoves as well as kitchens built to accommodate 2,000 men. But by the time the construction was completed, there were 6,000 men confined at Camp Parole.

On any given day or night, 50 to 2,000 parolees arrived from battlefields or rebel prison camps. They were usually ragged, sometimes shoeless and often covered with filth and vermin. They seldom had overcoats or blankets.

Sangster met this emergency by building eight wooden barracks, accommodating 150 men each, on the campus of St. John's College. Three of these were set aside for incoming prisoners. Two thousand complete suits and a like number of overcoats, pairs of shoes, blankets and sets of eating utensils were kept on hand; the new arrivals were provided with clothing and supplies only after they had discarded their old garments and had bathed thoroughly. Two or three days later they were transferred from the campus barracks to Camp Parole.

Frederick W. Wilde, an ex-prisoner who was assigned to Camp Parole, wrote some years later that "the mosquitoes were terrible at night, and the flies were worse, if possible, in the day." Wilde also observed: "We reported at the camp and found it very undesirable, and also found a worst pest than we had yet encountered as soldiers, namely Fleas! With a capital F. Of all the pests they were the most annoying."

A cavalry squadron of 35 men, known as the Purnell Legion, was billeted at the college barracks. These men maintained discipline at camp and were also designated as the regular guard. One of their duties was to ride regularly about the countryside in the vicinity of the camp on the lookout for deserters, stragglers and any soldiers who preyed on the community. Peaceful farmers and Annapolis merchants were frequently harassed by the unruly soldiers and Sangster attempted desperately to keep his men in line.

In his remembrance of his stay at Camp Parole, Wilde said the guards "were mostly boys and favored sons who had seen no active service in the field, or they would have been more sympathetic...." Wilde said he and his men were treated better by the Confederate guards when they were captured and sent to Belle Island prison near Richmond, Virginia. The rebel guards, he recalled, "were willing and often did share their rations with the prisoners."

Perhaps unaware of the inadequate number of guards at Parole, Wilde wrote: "I did not know at the time why the authorities were not more strict in regards to keeping the paroled prisoners in camp, later on, however, I heard it insinuated that the officers in charge kept on drawing money for the full amount of prisoners whether they were in camp or not."

In March of 1863, Captain H.M. Lazelle was dispatched by Colonel Hoffman, commissioner-general of prisoners for the Union Army, to inspect conditions at Camp Parole.

Lazelle's report praised Lieutenant Colonel Sangster for his efficiency and the improvements he made at the camp. But it was also noted that Sangster was severely handicapped by the lack of sufficient officers and guards to assist him. Lazelle's description of the accumulation of filth and rubbish in the camp led Colonel Hoffman to recommend that a new location for the prisoners be found. Sangster, who wanted the camp to be situated closer to a railroad track, agreed wholeheartedly.

Later the Federal Government signed a lease for the use of the nearby 250-acre Welch farm at a rent of $125 a month. Sixty frame barracks, each designed to house 120 men, were erected on the new site. In addition, two storehouses, 20 kitchens, each capable of feeding 400 men, and six hospital buildings were constructed. The construction of the new camp was done entirely by paroled soldiers, according to Sangster's reports; it seems more likely, however, that some Annapolis craftsmen helped with this enormous task. At any rate, the mule teams that had trudged back and forth from Annapolis to bring supplies for 6,000 to 7,000 men, were no longer needed.

A significant role in the life of Camp Parole was played by the band of the 114th Pennsylvania Volunteers, who had been captured and paroled at the Battle of Fredericksburg. Since their instruments had been confiscated by the music-loving rebels, the band members scraped together enough money from their own meager pay to buy new ones.

The band played at prisoner arrivals and departures and at all funerals. Sangster credited the band, which brought color and spirit into the drab monotony of the camp routine, with helping him to maintain discipline.

There are few recorded accounts of personal experiences at Camp Parole, but many years ago an old Annapolitan was found who remembered the camp from his boyhood. His most vivid recollection was that he once saw a soldier, who had been caught stealing, forced to march up and down before the entire camp one afternoon; pinned to the back of the prisoner's shirt was a large square cloth on which was printed in large black letters: THIEF.

During its entire existence, Camp Parole had under its charge as many as 70,000 men but probably never more than 8,000 at any one time. Although it is not known exactly when the camp was disbanded, one of the last references to it was found in a letter written on June 21, 1865 by Captain John Power, who was the commanding officer of the camp at the time. He wrote that the "business of the camp would be closed in two or three months."

It is known that the quartermaster stores including horses, wagons, carts, ambulances, harnesses, lumber, policing tools and even the barracks (each 104 feet by 25 feet and 10 feet high) were sold at public auction.

For many years after the army abandoned the camp, Parole was an important station for the once-thriving Baltimore and Annapolis Railroad since it was a way point for passengers leaving Annapolis for both Washington and Baltimore.

The Russian Sailor Incident

XV

THE RUSSIAN SAILOR INCIDENT

A Russian sailor was shot and killed by an Annapolis restaurant owner on February 4, 1864. While it might not have been a shot heard 'round the world, the concern in Washington was grave enough to place the ingenuity of American diplomacy into high gear.

The incident in Annapolis occurred at the very time when the Russian Government was making inexplicably friendly gestures toward the Union; these overtures were credited with effectively dissuading England and France from intervening in the American Civil War on behalf of the Confederacy.

There were economic advantages to be gained by England and France if the South could maintain a government independent of the North since the Dixie states had little industry but plenty of cotton and tobacco to export.

Two Russian warships, commanded by Admiral Lessovsky, unexpectedly arrived in New York harbor in mid-September of 1863. Two weeks later, three more Russian ships appeared. Simultaneously, six Russian warships under Admiral Popov, anchored in the harbor at San Francisco.

The Federal Government heartily welcomed the Russians. While Lessovsky took pains to avoid specific references as to the purpose of his visit, he demonstrated fervent sympathy for the Union cause. France and England feared that an alliance between the Union and the Russians had been made and quietly withdrew any further consideration of entering the war as an ally of the South.

In early December, Admiral Lessovsky sailed his squadron from New York harbor to Washington where he and his men were graciously received.

While it was originally believed that the visiting ships would spend the winter in the Severn River near Annapolis, this was officially disclaimed and later in the month the five vessels made their way to Hampton Roads, Virginia.

On January 29, 1864, two of the Russian ships, the *Variag* and the *Almas*, dropped anchor in the Severn abreast of the Naval Academy grounds, which were then being used as a hospital depot for Federal troops wounded in battle.

An Annapolis correspondent for a Baltimore newspaper described the two ships in the following manner:

"One is a sloop-of-war mounting eighteen guns, 64 pounders; the other is a gunboat, clipper model, bark-rigged, 320 feet long, mounting three heavy pivot guns and several howitzers on broadside. Both are beautiful, rakish-looking craft, and are fine specimens of the naval architecture of our powerful friends."

Upon their arrival, the Russian ships saluted the American flag with 21 guns and the Americans returned the honor gun for gun. It is interesting to note that the bandmaster aboard the *Almas* was Rimsky-Korsakov, later to become renowned as the composer of *Scheherazade*.

Six days after the arrival of the ships, a Russian sailor from the *Almas* named Demidoff, accompanied by a shipmate, went into an Annapolis saloon kept by John Moseley. The bartender apparently had strict orders from the owner to serve them nothing harder than cider. When the sailors demanded something with a bit more kick, like vodka, the bartender asked a Union cavalryman to escort them back to their ship.

Out on the street, the two seamen assaulted the American soldier who hastily took refuge in a nearby restaurant. The Russians followed but were unable to find him, so they attacked the restaurant proprietor. During the scuffle, the restaurateur's wife handed him a pistol which he used to fire the fatal shot into Demidoff.

The Russian Embassy in Washington was promptly notified and the Maryland Legislature, which happened to be in session, appointed a special committee to investigate the incident.

President Lincoln personally telegraphed Maryland Governor Augustus W. Bradford, requesting the full details surrounding the shooting. The restaurant owner had been taken into custody but was later released on $1,000 bail.

Two days after the incident occurred, funeral rites of the Russian Orthodox Church were held for Demidoff at the United States Naval Academy. The funeral was attended by high-ranking United States Navy and Army officers, a representative of the Russian Embassy, and officers from the two Russian warships. After the service, the body was carried by Demidoff's shipmates to the National Cemetery in Annapolis where he was buried.

The *Variag* and the *Almas* remained in the Severn throughout the winter. The Maryland Legislature appointed a seven-member committee to visit the warships. After an exchange of 21-gun salutes, there were toasts honoring the Emperor and Empress of Russia, the Governor of Maryland and the Maryland General Assembly.

When warm weather arrived, Admiral Lessovsky's fleet, including the two ships anchored at Annapolis, returned home.

While the visit of the Russian ships was considered by the United States for many years as an outstanding demonstration of friendship, an American historian, Professor A.F. Golder, viewed the matter in a somewhat different light.

After laboriously sifting through the archives of the Russian Minister of Marine, the professor concluded that the Russians were acting in their own selfish interests. At the time, England had been disturbed by Russian military intervention to put down disturbances in Poland and was threatening to declare war on Russia. Golder believed the actual purpose of the Russian vessels visiting New York and San Francisco was to establish strategic positions in friendly ice-free ports where they could attack British commercial ships in the event that war erupted.

Professor Golder's plausible theory notwithstanding, the timely appearance of the Russian ships when the Union desperately needed all the help it could muster, was reciprocated by the reluctance of the U.S. State Department to recognize the fall of the czarist regime in 1919.

A reminder of the visit of the Russian ships is found in the National Cemetery in Annapolis where a headstone is marked with the following inscription:

"N. Demidoff, Seaman of the Russian Sloop-of-War *Almas,* killed at Annapolis, February 4, 1864."

XVI

RED CARPET PRISONERS

The naval lieutenant was befuddled.

Lieutenant W.S. Benson's assignment seemed simple enough on that hot 16th day of July in 1898; but he was encountering unexpected difficulty in carrying it out.

Armed with a sheaf of papers, Lieutenant Benson had dutifully marched down to the Santee Wharf at the Naval Academy and awaited the arrival of a ship bearing 79 Spanish naval and marine officers captured at Santiago. His mission was merely to obtain the signatures of the officers on their individual parole sheets which were carefully made out in both Spanish and English.

The lieutenant's dilemma began when the ranking Spanish officer, Admiral Pascal Cervera y Topete, refused to sign.

Evidently the Admiral was still smarting over his recent defeat. After Commodore George Dewey demolished most of the Spanish fleet at Manila Bay, Cervera, who was anchored in Santiago harbor on the southern coast of Cuba, had been in command of practically all that remained of the Spanish Navy. With the U.S. North Atlantic fleet blockading the harbor and American troops landing a few miles east of Santiago, Cervera was in imminent danger of being caught between the crossfire of ground forces and naval vessels. On July 3, he attempted to run the blockade and save his ships by steaming out of the harbor. The decision proved disastrous; every Spanish ship was either sunk or beached.

And now Cervera was being asked to suffer yet another humiliation. The Admiral dismissed the matter of signing his parole sheet by informing Lieutenant Benson that the word of one officer and gentleman to another should be sufficient. Furthermore, he saw no reason why his junior officers should be subjected to the indignity of signing anything either. And they did not.

Eventually the officers relented and signed their paroles with the exception of Captain Antonio Eulate, captain of the *Vizcaya*. Because of his stubbornness, the captain was temporarily detained within the Naval Academy walls while the other officers were free to roam Annapolis almost at will. However, Naval Academy Superintendent McNair could see no reason why Captain Eulate, signature or no, could not be out on the streets of Annapolis with his brother officers and this privilege was extended to him as well.

Eulate, who had suffered back and head wounds at Santiago, was despondent and paranoid. He was frequently heard to comment that he had lost all "but my commission and my honor." Fearing that he would be poisoned by his Yankee captors, the captain insisted that an American orderly test his food before he would sit down to a meal.

Moreover, Eulate, upon learning that San Juan had been taken by the Americans, became deeply concerned about the safety and welfare of his wife and children. Although he somewhat emerged from his shell when he was assured his family was secure, Captain Eulate remained a generally lonely and dejected man.

It was only natural for some of the Spaniards to fear the worst when they were captured. At the time Mellado, paymaster of the *Almirante Oquendo*, was taken prisoner, he was clutching a small metal box. He told Lieutenant Commander Harry P. Huse that he preferred death to surrendering the box. Huse asked Mellado for his word that there was nothing in it that might be of value to the United States Government. Mellado gave his word.

The contents of the box were revealed several weeks later to someone the paymaster befriended during his captivity in Annapolis: a packet of letters from his wife and water-soaked photographs of his family.

Annapolis welcomed the Spanish officers with a spirit of cordiality seldom approached between citizens of warring nations. Admiral Cervera set an example of dignity and adaptability. The Spaniards went so far as to salute along with the American officers whenever The Stars and Stripes were raised or lowered.

Only once was this atmosphere of amicability threatened. Four days after Admiral Cervera and his group arrived, another ship reached Annapolis with 34 additional prisoners who told of a shipboard massacre in which six Spanish seamen were killed and several others were wounded.

What had happened turned out to be a tragic mistake. The prisoners could not understand English; their confusion in attempting to obey orders was misinterpreted by American soldiers guarding them as an attempted uprising. The soldiers responded by firing into the Spanish prisoners.

Although Admiral Cervera was gravely concerned about the stupidity of the soldiers, he accepted the unfortunate incident as a by-product of the tensions of war and he did not hold it against the Americans.

The young ladies of Annapolis and the Naval Academy were especially overjoyed by the arrival of the Spanish officers. With their own beaux off fighting in the war, they were lonesome for male companionship and they were intrigued by the dashing appearance and charming manners of the newcomers. The Spanish officers were pleasantly surprised by the relative freedom of young American women, even in 1898; they were much more accessible than the chaperoned señoritas back home. Consequently, the young ladies learned Spanish and the officers learned English, or at least enough to facilitate fraternization.

If a young Annapolis lady admired a possession of one of the Spaniards, he would gallantly offer it to her. The gold diggers and souvenir hunters among the fairer sex were quick to take advantage of these chivalrous gestures and began collecting watches, rings and other trinkets at a furious pace.

One particularly handsome and well-bred young officer was especially popular with the damsels of Annapolis. He wrote home about the splendid time he was having and apparently devoted much of his correspondence to a certain attractive young daughter of an American officer.

The Spaniard's mother wired Admiral Cervera, "Send Luis home immediately!" As congenial as his "imprisonment" was, Luis was still not quite in a position to catch the next boat back to sunny Spain. However, the young officer eventually returned home a single man, leaving behind an untold number of broken hearts, and he later rose to a prominent position in the Spanish Government.

By the end of August, word came from Washington that the prisoners were to be returned. While the news disheartened a segment of Annapolis' female population, it did not particularly disturb those American officers who had returned from tedious blockade duty to find their daughters entertaining enemy officers in their own parlors.

Upon departing Annapolis, Admiral Cervera profusely thanked Superintendent McNair for his gracious hospitality and, once aboard ship, the Admiral telegraphed further expressions of appreciation to McNair.

There were more than a few regrets among the departing Spanish officers, some of whom would have gladly extended their stay as red carpet prisoners in charming Annapolis. Although there were many brief romances, no marriages are known to have resulted from this curious chapter in the history of Annapolis.

The Last Captive

XVII

THE LAST CAPTIVE

During the closing weeks of the Spanish-American War, all but one of the several Spanish prisoners who had been held in Annapolis were returned home. The United States Government refused to release a prisoner named Cristobal, who was confined behind bars at the Naval Academy until he died some ten years after he was captured.

Cristobal Colon was the parrot mascot of the Spanish cruiser *Colon* that ran up on the Santiago harbor beach aflame during Admiral Cervera's abortive effort to smash the American blockade on July 3, 1898.

While Americans were rescuing the wounded from the burning vessel, a dying Spanish officer pointed to the bowsprit where Cristobal stood, a sorry sight with all his feathers scorched away and squawking ferociously.

Before the officer died, he implored an American midshipman to send Cristobal to someone who would take care of him. The midshipman decided to keep the parrot himself.

A short while later, Cristobal said to the midshipman, "Da me un besito" meaning "Give me a kiss" and when the midshipman leaned forward to accept the parrot's affection, the bird stabbed his new master with his sharp beak.

The incident resulted in Cristobal finding himself behind the bars of a locked cage. Anxious to rid himself of the vicious bird, the midshipman wrote a letter to the daughter of an officer he knew at the Naval Academy explaining that he was sending her a pet that had once belonged to a Spanish naval officer.

A week after she received the letter, the young lady became acquainted with Cristobal quite by accident. She happened to be in the express office in Annapolis when she noticed a parrot in a cage. The one-eyed featherless bird had bitterly chewed up most of his tag, leaving only the words "Annapolis, Md." The express office manager had no idea what to do with the parrot and was probably relieved when the young lady claimed it.

Shortly after taking possession of Cristobal, the young woman nearly lost the tip of her finger when she attempted to befriend him. Cristobal knew nothing of the celebrated Spanish chivalry; as far as he was concerned, the enemy was the enemy and the mere sound of an American accent was enough to send him into a temper tantrum.

One day a Spaniard happened to be passing the veranda where Cristobal was, as usual, confined securely within his birdcage. "Papa! Papa!" screeched the parrot. The Spaniard rushed up to the veranda and opened the cage. "Da me un besito!" cried Cristobal, as he lovingly nestled his beak against his countryman's face. The Spaniard explained that he had been the cook aboard the *Colon* and that Cristobal had been entrusted to his care.

The cook frequently returned with an ear of corn which Cristobal hungrily devoured. Each time he returned, their little love ritual was repeated. But when the cook and the other prisoners were returned to Spain, the U.S. Naval Department callously ruled that no pets could be taken aboard.

Thus, Cristobal, the only Spanish prisoner who vociferously voiced his discontent with the circumstances of his imprisonment in Annapolis, was destined to remain on foreign soil.

Whenever he saw his beloved Spanish flag, Cristobal would imitate a cheer. But mostly he would maintain an ominous, brooding silence except to mock the voices in the household where he was kept. He rolled his single portside eye with such a hostile expression that strangers did not have to be warned twice to keep their distance.

When Cristobal died about a decade after the Battle of Santiago (and almost on the anniversary of that event), nearly an entire column was devoted to his obituary in the *New York Herald*.

And so, a parrot, who carried his nationalistic fervor to the point of nastiness, was the last physical reminder of the Spanish naval officers who once roamed Annapolis streets, making friends and showing Americans there can be dignity even in defeat.

XVIII

NIGHTINGALE IN A HENCOOP

Professor Marshall Oliver seems to have been entirely out of place as a member of the United States Naval Academy faculty during the turn of the nineteenth century. A short-tempered, arrogant individual, he made no effort to conceal his intense dislike for the Navy.

In fact, this handsome man who wore a monocle and a waxed moustache and who had the carriage of a pompous aristocrat was fond of letting people know that while he was in the Navy he was not part of it; he held great pride in that difference. When he was introduced to someone, he stood with his heels together and one arm crooked behind his back in the manner of a European nobleman.

Professor Oliver considered himself above his colleagues on the faculty as well as even the highest ranking Naval officers. He was bored by what he considered to be the Philistine atmosphere of the Academy with the incessant cackling about promotions, the latest Washington gossip, uniforms, regulations and official reports. He seemed to believe his presence in Annapolis was only a temporary situation and that a higher calling awaited someone of his obvious culture, talents and brilliance. Describing his plight at the Academy, the professor would refer to himself as "a nightingale in a hencoop."

He frequently told the midshipmen: "There are three accomplishments every gentleman should have—fencing, music and languages." Then, thumping his chest for dramatic emphasis, he would add, "I have all three."

It was said that Oliver studied art in Paris as a young man and that, for a time, he was a member of the artists' colony in Florence which included American and British painters, sculptors, writers and poets, among whom were Robert and Elizabeth Barrett Browning.

There was even a legend about his friendship with Browning. Supposedly, Professor Oliver and the poet were once walking together on the banks of the Arno River when Oliver spotted a piece of timber, rapped it with his walking stick and remarked that it would make an excellent violin. Weeks later, the story goes, Browning sent Oliver a violin made from that piece of wood, accompanied by a note expressing the hope that some day his son might have the opportunity to play the instrument.

When Oliver returned to the United States, he became an actor in New York and managed to obtain a part in a production of *Richelieu* with the great Edwin Booth in the title role.

Apparently unable to earn a decent living as either an artist or an actor, Oliver came to the Naval Academy where he was placed on the faculty as an instructor of drawing. As a member of the commissioned corps of professors, he was entitled to wear the uniform of the United States Navy which he held in such low regard.

When freehand drawing was dropped from the Academy curriculum, he instructed mechanical drawing and obviously felt it was far beneath him to teach his subject with the use of compasses, triangles and rulers.

His wife seemed as much of a nonconformist as the professor. She ignored the pompadour hairstyle of her day and wore her own hair parted in the middle while large golden hoops dangled from her earlobes.

Their home, with its music and books, was a sanctuary from the Academy life that impressed neither of them.

Despite the fact that they had traveled abroad, the Olivers were distrustful of the Spanish prisoners who were brought to Annapolis after the Battle of Santiago and allowed to roam freely through the town and the grounds of the Naval Academy. They insinuated that the Spanish officers were capable of committing the most heinous crimes, including murder, and they advised against wandering on the Academy grounds after dark.

The Spaniards were aware of the Olivers' feelings, but seemed to understand them. The Spanish officers were also extremely fond of music and they often gathered on the porches of the Olivers' neighbors on Upshur Road to listen to the sounds of melodic voices and instruments coming from the windows of the eccentric professor's home.

While Professor Oliver had little respect for the Navy, it was obvious the Navy had a considerable amount of respect for him. He was appointed architect of the Academy chapel and was called upon to draw plans for a new science building. His abilities as a linguist and his knowledge of books were also recognized when he was appointed to serve as Naval Academy librarian, a position he held from 1895 to 1899.

For the rest of his life, this fiery dilettante remained at the Naval Academy, where he felt even those few who had even heard of Browning and Booth were unable to appreciate their accomplishments. Marshall Oliver, the self-styled "nightingale in a hencoop," was buried with the full military honors that are traditionally extended to ranking officers.

XIX

THE GHOSTS OF BRICE HOUSE

The most chilling ghost tales related in Annapolis many years ago were associated with the Brice House, the handsome colonial mansion on the corner of Prince George and East streets.

In the nineteenth century, the last of the Brices was found dead in his library. It was not certain whether the wound on the old gentleman's head was inflicted by a blunt object or whether he struck it on the floor after suffering from a stroke. However, the disappearance of his valet led to the popular conclusion that Mr. Brice's death was the result of foul play. As the years passed, it was widely believed that the ghosts of the murdered man and his assailant periodically reenacted the crime within the stately old house.

During the first three decades of the twentieth century, several occupants of Brice House reported strange occurrences at the mansion. Noises were heard in the walls and one witness to these eerie sounds described them as "a regular sort of knocking; something like the Morse Code."

One young man who occupied a room on the top floor of the house claimed he was startled one morning by what might have been the ghost of Mr. Brice's murderer. When the intruder turned to leave the room, the young man jumped out of his bed and followed closely behind him. But when they reached the hallway, the "ghost" disappeared.

On another occasion, a Naval Academy professor, who resided on the ground floor, left his room at 7:30 one morning on his way to an 8 a.m. class. Passing the door to the library, the professor confronted a white-haired gentleman standing at the threshold wearing a black stocking cap and attired in a black suit. There, before the professor's eyes, the old gentleman "gradually melted out of sight like a mist."

The professor was reportedly not a drinking man but a level-headed person whose word was supposedly unimpeachable; he claimed that the night before he witnessed the apparition he retired at ten thirty. A naval officer's wife and her daughter also claimed to have seen the same, old white-haired gentleman dressed in black, but were reluctant to discuss it further.

Another bizarre episode connected with the Brice House unfolded after the mansion was purchased as a private residence. During the renovation of the walls, a closet was revealed that had been hidden by plaster. Inside the closet was the skeleton of a woman.

There were rumors that a woman in the Brice family was insane and, because at that time insanity was considered to be a great personal

The Ghosts of Brice House

disgrace, she was secretly confined in the house. There is a theory that she was entombed in the wall so that no one would learn of her existence.

In more recent years, occupants of the Brice House have not reported any ghosts in the house and the legend that the place is haunted has faded gradually with the passage of time.

XX

THE UNFLAPPABLE COLONEL OF MARYLAND AVENUE

No gallery of authentic town characters from Annapolis' past would be complete that does not include Colonel Tilton, who always spoke his mind and usually left his audience both stunned and smiling.

A widower and onetime commander of the city's Marine Barracks, the colonel remained in Annapolis long after his retirement from the military. Around the turn of the century, he resided in a yellow brick house on Maryland Avenue near the Naval Academy gate.

Colonel Tilton possessed a number of priceless eccentricities that were obviously outgrowths of his delightful sense of the ridiculous. Ample evidence of these traits could be found in the adornments of his home.

On the hatstand near the front door were a number of faded sunbonnets which must have aroused the curiosity of first-time visitors to the abode of an old gentleman living alone; he never deemed it necessary to explain the bonnets to anyone. Gracing the front window of the home was a plaster rendering of the Venus de Milo, unfrocked during the warmer months but snugly clad in a small knitted garment during the winter. Shaving balls, which had been gifts from young ladies, hung from the living-room chandelier.

Among the colonel's favorite pastimes was entertaining young damsels at breakfast. They would arrive in groups at ten o'clock in the morning and begin with oatmeal, but the dessert was sometimes served as late as four o'clock. Between courses, at the colonel's insistence, all the guests would go outdoors and run around the house to stimulate their appetites.

Never one to mince words, Colonel Tilton was particularly free with his advice to the young ladies in matters of the social graces. They, in turn, would express their appreciation for sharing his bountiful wisdom by constantly showering him with gifts—slippers, bedsocks, pincushions and, of course, shaving balls.

Once when he offered his arm to a young woman who accepted it too enthusiastically for his taste, the colonel told her, "You should light on me like a crow, not a canary." He frequently counseled his distaff admirers to "say what you will, but don't write letters."

The colonel had an obsession about cleanliness. When his underwear would return from the laundress, he would immediately soak them in his washtub and scrub them again with his own hands.

He was once vigorously engaged in this activity upstairs in his house when he heard the doorbell and called for his visitors to come right up.

They did, and the colonel found himself (up to his elbows in soapsuds) face to face with the Governor of Maryland who was accompanied by his personal entourage. The colonel calmly reached for his towel, dried his hands, put on his shirt and led the party downstairs without revealing even the slightest tinge of embarrassment.

Before automobiles came to the streets of Annapolis, Colonel Tilton was fond of taking brisk walks around and about town; but, scorning the sidewalks, he always insisted upon striding directly up the middle of the street where approaching carriages yielded the right of way.

While taking one of his daily constitutionals, the colonel once greeted a friend with: "Good morning to you. Do you know that your intestines are twenty-eight and one-half feet long?" Before the friend could respond to this sudden outburst of information, the colonel added, "That's just how long they are." Then he continued his journey up the middle of the street.

The only evidence of his humor ever bordering on the macabre was the amusement he derived from telling visitors that he kept his coffin under his bed. What he actually kept there was a silver chest.

Colonel Tilton's greatest pleasure seemed to be in catching people by surprise, but he always managed to do it in a rather charming, tongue-in-cheek manner. The lovable old gentleman kept a generation of his Annapolis friends and neighbors both amused and amazed. He was truly an Annapolis original.

XXI

THE SPINSTERS' PRIDE

Visitors to the Hammond-Harwood House in Annapolis are told of the romantic legend of Matthias Hammond, the tragic bachelor who built the elegant mid-eighteenth-century home for his fiancée but was jilted because she believed he cared more for the new house than he did for her.

Perhaps equally as interesting were the fiercely proud Harwood sisters, who, many years later, were the last occupants of the home that is considered one of the most outstanding examples of American colonial architecture. The spinster sisters rarely permitted anyone inside the doors of this splendid home which is now open to the public. They were known to chase away inquisitive architects who climbed a wall behind the house, risking limb if not life, to sketch the magnificent interior designed by the renowned William Buckland.

William Harwood, a professor of English and Ethics at the Naval Academy, became master of the house in the 1850's. At the outbreak of the Civil War, his outspoken allegiance was with the Confederacy. He is said to have departed from the Academy in a most flamboyant fashion; he supposedly spread out an American flag at the main gate, jumped up and down upon it, and shouted derogatory opinions about President Lincoln and the Federal Government. According to the legend, the marine guarding the gate grabbed Harwood and threw him into the street.

The highly opinionated professor subsequently obtained a teaching post at a school near Baltimore. But he adamantly refused to swear the oath of allegiance to the Union that was required from those passengers riding the train between Annapolis and Baltimore.

He chose instead to walk the 30 miles over rugged dirt roads to Baltimore at the beginning of every week; at the end of the week, he trudged back to Annapolis on foot.

Following the war, Harwood remained in the house with his two daughters until he grew too old to teach. His daughters, Miss Lucy and Miss Hester, sheltered him from the knowledge of their impoverished state.

However, they always seemed to find enough money to file a seemingly endless procession of lawsuits. Particularly upsetting to them was the fact that the Chase Home, directly across the street from the Hammond-Harwood House, was deeded to the Episcopal Church as a residence for elderly ladies. The Harwood sisters, granddaughters of Judge Jeremiah Townley Chase to whom Hammond sold the home shortly after it was completed, refused to have anything to do with anyone who ascended the steps of the Chase Home.

After their father died, Miss Lucy and Miss Hester continued to reside in their house, refusing to part with the priceless antique furnishings although they literally did not know where their next meal was coming from.

Sympathetic neighbors would place baskets of food at their door while the sisters watched from the windows. While they would take the baskets, the Harwood sisters would snub these same neighbors whenever they passed them on the street.

While strolling in the garden behind their house, the spinsters were frequently taunted by mischievous neighborhood boys. Miss Lucy would rush back into the house and return brandishing a formidable oversized dueling pistol with which she threatened to shoot the youngsters.

When she was young, Miss Hester was said to have been in love with a midshipman attending the Naval Academy. However, her older and domineering sister, who was never known to have a suitor, supposedly discovered a letter from the midshipman that began, "My darling Hessie." Miss Lucy saw to it that the young man never again attempted to court the younger Harwood sister.

Miss Hester was left alone in the house when Miss Lucy, said to be at least 100 years old, died. Neighbors were convinced the cause of her death was starvation rather than old age.

After leaving Annapolis for several months, Miss Hester returned and frequently was seen wearing the old family jewelry as well as a new set of false teeth. However, none of the well-known Harwood pride had diminished. Finding herself in violent disagreement with her attorney, she once wrote him a letter of dismissal in the strongest language she could summon; instead of mailing it, Miss Hester charged into his office, deposited the letter at his feet, wheeled around, stormed out of the door, slammed it behind her and never spoke a single word.

Remaining in the house, she began speaking of her onetime lover. Upon discovering someone of the same name on the list of the Board of Visitors of the Naval Academy, she was certain her suitor of long ago had returned and was still true to her. She also convinced herself that she would have no more financial problems because he would take care of such bothersome details for her. In her final days, she tore up her will and began talking to him in nightly visions.

Long after Miss Hester died, Dr. James E. Boardley, who headed the committee in charge of restoring the old house, spotted two loose bricks in the cellar. He worked them free and discovered two large keys, tagged respectively in faded ink: "To the Secret Chamber" and "To the Secret Burying Place."

Since all the Harwoods were accounted for in various cemeteries, the keys loomed as an immense mystery. A possible clue evolved when an Annapolis woman recalled that Miss Hester, on her deathbed, mentioned that she would take a great secret to her grave.

Later, an elderly lady residing in Baltimore claimed that as a girl she often played with the Harwood sisters and she remembered a secret passage in the house. She said the passage was reached from stairs to the cellar and that it led underground to a little brook at the rear of the garden. The woman from Baltimore also insisted that en route to the brook one passed a tomb.

There was another legend that the woman who had broken her engagement to Matthias Hammond had pleaded, as her final wish, to be buried in the garden of the house that had been built as her wedding gift.

Although there was some excavation in an effort to unravel this intriguing puzzle, neither the tunnel nor the tomb was ever located.

Miss Hester's death and the fact that she tore up her will left the Hammond-Harwood House without an heir.

Antique dealers and wealthy collectors crowded the inside and outside of the house shouting their bids for the valuable antiques that were auctioned to whomever would pay the highest price. A Sheraton sideboard sold for $1,200; a table went for $700; chairs brought between $180 and $300 each.

There were those observing the auction who felt the strange irony of the determination of Miss Lucy and Miss Hester to starve rather than part with these great household treasures; in their resolve, the Harwood spinsters were true, throughout their lives, to the legacy of indomitable pride inherited from their unrelenting father.

Mark Twain's Visit to Annapolis

XXII

MARK TWAIN'S VISIT TO ANNAPOLIS

If this nation paid proper respect to its great men of letters, November 30 would be a most significant date on our calendar. On that date, back in 1835 in the town of Florida, Missouri, Mark Twain was born.

Although Twain died in 1910, he is survived by the two most beloved characters in American fiction—Huck Finn and Tom Sawyer.

The Twain legacy also includes a number of essays, short stories and books, among which *Life on the Mississippi* and *Roughing It* rate alongside *The Adventures of Huckleberry Finn* and *The Adventures of Tom Sawyer* as American classics.

He was one of those rare literary giants who was as adept at dispensing the spoken word as he was with the written word.

With his outstanding stage presence and his brilliant sense of timing, Twain developed the telling of tall tales into a widely acclaimed art. The popular demand for Twain on the lecture circuit brought him to Annapolis on May 11, 1907. He was introduced to his audience by Governor Edwin Warfield.

Following his performance, Twain told a *New York Times* reporter that he was nearly arrested while touring the grounds of the United States Naval Academy.

"Mine was no ordinary offense," he insisted. "When I affront the law I choose to do so in no obscure, insignificant, trivial manner. Mine was a crime against nothing less than the Federal Government. The officers who arrested me were no common, or garden, policemen; they were clothed with the authority of the Federal Constitution. I was charged with smoking a cigar within a Government reservation. In fact, I was caught red-handed. I came near setting a stone pile on fire.

"It is true that the arrest was not made effective. One of the party whispered to the marines what Governor Warfield was going to say, and did say, in introducing me to the audience at my lecture—that I was one of the greatest men in the world. I don't know who proposed to tell that to the marines, but it worked like a charm. The minions of the law faltered, hesitated, quailed, and today I am a free man."

Twain said he could not decide for certain whether or not he was worthy of Governor Warfield's compliment, adding:

> "But who am I to contradict the Governor of Maryland? Worm that I am, by what right should I traverse the declared opinion of that man of wisdom and judgment whom I have learned to admire and trust?

"I never admired him more than I did when he told the audience that they had with them the greatest man in the world. I believe that was his expression. I don't wish to undertake his sentiments, but I will go no further than that—at present. Why, it fairly warmed my heart. It almost made me glad to be there myself. I like good company."

Twain told the reporter he was "much impressed by the Naval Academy. I was all over it, and now it is all over me. I am full of the navy. I wanted to march with them, but they didn't think to ask me; curious inattention on their part...."

The celebrated author also told the correspondent that his illicit cigar smoking on government property "was not the first time I ever did wrong."

He said that back in Hannibal, Missouri, at the age of 13, he stole a watermelon from a farmer's wagon only to learn later that his purloined contraband was unripened. He returned the stolen item to the farmer and scolded him for giving his customers green melons.

"And he was ashamed," Twain said. "He said he was. He said he felt as badly about it as I did. In this he was mistaken. He hadn't eaten any of the melon."

Upon reflection, Twain said, it was "one of the gratifications of my life that I can look back on what I did for that man in his hour of need."

The farmer gave him a ripe melon and went home to his wife with a clear conscience, according to Twain.

"Reform with me was no transient emotion, no passing episode.... It was permanent," the renowned humorist commented. "Since that day I have never stolen a water ... never stolen a green watermelon."

Rudyard Kipling once quoted Twain as saying: "Get your facts first, and then you can distort them as much as you please."

During his brief stay in Annapolis, Twain proved that he adhered tenaciously to that principle.

Twain's final public appearance was in Catonsville, Maryland, on June 10, 1909, when he delivered the commencement address at St. Timothy's School for young ladies.

Prior to delivering his address, he stayed overnight in Baltimore. There he met with newsmen and had agreeable things to say about everything from the unique excellence of Baltimore fried chicken (the ultimate compliment from an authority on the South where that culinary delicacy had been perfected) to the stimulating influence of Baltimore's beautiful women (a supreme compliment from a celebrated world traveler and professional observer).

The 73-year-old writer was so moved by Baltimore's amiable atmosphere that he told the press, "I am just as young now as I was forty years ago. Why, I don't see any reason why I shouldn't live for another hundred years." And, as if to emphasize his sincerity, he added: "There's nothing funny about that."

In his speech to the young ladies at St. Timothy's, he illustrated that honesty is the best policy by recounting in his drawling, elaborate, embroidering fashion, an incident he claimed happened to him as a young man.

It seemed that Twain and his friend William Swinton had established what he declared was "the first newspaper syndicate on the planet." They became the Washington correspondents for 12 weekly newspapers, "all obscure and poor and all scattered far away among the back settlements," according to Twain's autobiography. Each of the newspapers purchased two columns a week at the price of one dollar per column; but there came a time when the two correspondents ran short of money and desperately needed the sum of three dollars.

After wandering the streets of Washington, Twain went into the lobby of the then new Ebbitt House hotel and sat down to rest. He was approached by a friendly dog. While Twain was stroking the dog's head and fondling the animal's droopy ears, a Brigadier General Miles came up and asked him if he would consider selling the pet; Twain said he would. The general asked the price and Twain replied, "Three dollars." Expressing surprise, the general said he wouldn't take a hundred dollars for such an outstanding dog and advised him to reconsider the price. "No, three dollars. That is his price," said Twain. The general gave him that amount and took the dog.

Ten minutes later a worried-looking man entered the lobby and began peering under the tables and chairs. Twain asked if he was looking for a dog and the man said he was. Twain told him he saw the dog follow a gentleman and that he might be able to locate him. The man said he would gladly pay him ten dollars if he could recover his pet; but Twain said he wanted only three dollars.

After consulting the hotel clerk, Twain visited the general's room and told him he needed the dog "because the man wants him again," explaining that "the man" was the dog's owner. The general couldn't believe he had sold another man's dog. Twain reminded him that he was not anxious to sell the animal, had not even thought of selling him, but did so as an "accommodation" to the general. The general was astounded by Twain's audacity. Twain recalled that the general himself said the dog was worth more than $100 and had offered to pay more, that the price was fair considering he didn't even own the animal, and asked the general to put himself in his place.

The exasperated general returned the dog and Twain gave back his three dollars. Then Twain returned the dog to its rightful owner and collected three dollars for his trouble.

"I went away then with a good conscience," Twain commented, "because I had acted honorably; I never could have used the three that I sold the dog for because it was not rightly my own, but the three I got for restoring him to his rightful owner was righteously and properly mine because I had earned it. That man might never have gotten that dog back at all if it hadn't been for me."

Twain concluded: "Now then, that is the tale. Some of it is true."

The highly esteemed author-lecturer further amused the girls at St. Timothy's with a brief list of useful precepts:

"There are three things . . . which I consider excellent advice. First, girls, don't smoke—to excess. I am 73½ years old and have been smoking 73 of them. But I never smoke to excess—that is, I smoke in moderation, only one cigar at a time. Also, never drink—to excess. Third, don't marry—to excess."

After he distributed diplomas to the graduation class, Twain adjourned to the lawn, lighted a black cigar and patiently endured posing for a seemingly endless procession of amateur photographers.

Approached by a newsman for an interview, he wearily said, "No, I have nothing to say worthwhile. People are constantly expecting me to say . . . clever and brilliant things. But that is . . . hard to do unless one has some inspiration. . . . You can't always say beautiful things at random. This morning I got inspiration for my address from the beautiful girls and the flowers and the harmonious surroundings."

While staying overnight in Baltimore prior to making his final public appearance, Twain complained of an odd, persistent pain in his chest—the first sympton of the angina that caused his death 11 months later.

XXIII

THE PLOT TO STEAL THE NAVAL ACADEMY

By the mid-1940's, Annapolitans had been accustomed to rumors that the Naval Academy would be removed from their city. Since 1915, bills had been regularly introduced in the United States Congress that were aimed at placing the Academy elsewhere or, at least, to establish a second Naval Academy on the West Coast.

However, in the summer of 1945 the Annapolis Chamber of Commerce felt the threat to "steal" the Academy was serious enough to express its fears to Maryland Governor Herbert R. O'Conor.

Only a few months earlier, Governor O'Conor had learned from President Franklin D. Roosevelt that plans were already on the drawing board for a second Naval Academy on the West Coast. In the President's opinion, there was absolutely nothing that could be done to curb the move. There were natural fears in Maryland that if a second Academy were to be built, Congress would eventually reach the conclusion that it would be economically unfeasible for the federal government to maintain both institutions and the one established in Annapolis in 1845 might well be destined for extinction.

By the time the Chamber of Commerce came to Governor O'Conor with its request to intervene on behalf of saving the original Naval Academy, the nation was under new leadership. President Roosevelt, who had once unsuccessfully attempted to enlist O'Conor's support for his effort to "pack" the U.S. Supreme Court so that it would rule favorably on the constitutionality of New Deal legislation, was dead.

Harry S. Truman, the former Senator from Missouri elected as President Roosevelt's running mate the previous year, was now in the White House. O'Conor had been a favorite-son candidate on the first ballot for the vice-presidential nomination at the 1944 Democratic National Convention in Chicago. Still fresh in Truman's memory was how O'Conor had led the switch to support him on the second ballot. The ensuing rush to the Truman bandwagon enabled the Missouri senator to wrest the vice-presidential nomination from incumbent Henry A. Wallace; Truman had trailed Wallace by the margin of 110 votes on the initial ballot.

A consummate politician who understood the necessity of repaying political debts, Truman was sympathetic to O'Conor's eloquent appeal to thwart the "unthinkable" effort "to uproot this historic institution and move it to another state."

The problem confronting O'Conor and Marylanders committed to retaining the Academy in Annapolis was that the Navy simply needed more space for this facility. Because St. John's College was having financial difficulties, the federal government had taken an option on that school's property after World War II began.

In the event that St. John's College would be forced to close or leave Annapolis, the city fathers had considered condemning one and one-third acres of the campus to build housing for naval personnel. But the Navy moved in and extracted an agreement from the college for first option on the property, subject to the State of Maryland's waiver of its right to the four central acres which would revert to the state in the event that the college had to be relocated.

The feeling in Annapolis, where 2,650 local workers were employed by the Academy, was that if it came down to a choice between the Academy and St. John's College, the old liberal arts institution would be the loser. Representatives of the International Brotherhood of Firemen and Oilers even told Governor O'Conor that St. John's, although it was one of the oldest institutions of higher learning in the nation, had "very, very little cultural value."

Maryland's two United States Senators took different views of the matter. Senator Millard Tydings was perfectly willing to bow to the Navy's wishes, while Senator George Radcliffe was vitally interested in saving St. John's College.

Eventually Governor O'Conor sided with those who did not believe it was necessary to sacrifice St. John's in order to keep the Naval Academy. And Marylanders received valuable support from Representative Carl Vinson, who radically opposed any attempts to create a second Naval Academy. As Chairman of the House Naval Affairs Committee, Vinson was, at that time, one of the most powerful figures in the United States Congress.

By filling in the Severn River and adjacent low-lying areas, the Navy was able to expand Academy facilities to the north and west. It was expensive, but not nearly as high as the price of establishing a second Naval Academy. Interestingly enough, the Academy now maintains a graduate school at Monterey, California.

And, of great significance to local preservationists, St. John's College eventually received a huge monetary gift that enabled the college to continue and prosper as an outstanding Great Books curriculum school.

Thus, the plot to steal the Naval Academy was smashed and the story has a happy ending—at least from the Annapolis point of view.